11th Edition

OPEN
SOURCE INDIA
NIMHANS Convention Center | BENGALURU

7 - 8
November
2014

OSI Curtain Raiser
Open Source India 2014 -11th Edition:
A FOSS Event You Just Can't Miss!

CW00431005

OpenSource

Volume: 03 | Issue: 02

THE COMPLETE MAGAZINE ON OPEN SOURCE

ForYou

An *EFY* GROUP Publication

HARNESS
THE POWER OF
THE CLOUD

Automate The Provisioning Of Cloud Inventory

Deploy Infrastructure-as-a-Service Using OpenStack

 **LIFERAY**®

Give web visitors
what they're looking for

BUILD A SOLUTION THAT WILL DELIGHT YOUR AUDIENCE AND DELIVER LONG-TERM VALUE

Enterprise

Liferay is the premier open source portal for the enterprise and satisfies market demands for a light, flexible portal platform across multiple industries.

Open Source

In development since 2000, Liferay Portal has become the world's most popular open source portal platform. It has over 5 million total downloads and a community of over 100,000 users.

For Life

Liferay supports non-profits around the world because we realize that life is more than just about making great open source software. It's about building communities for long term impact.

Try it for yourself:

Liferay Portal 6.2 features over 70 tools for portal, content, and collaboration.
Download and install in just 20 minutes. *https://www.liferay.com/products/liferay-portal/ee/30-day-trial*

Some of our customers...

 www.liferay.com
www.facebook.com/liferay
www.twitter.com/liferay

Liferay India Pvt Ltd
Alfa Center, Ground Floor,
Double Road Indiranagar
2nd stage, Bangalore -560038
Tel : +91 080 45445445 / 41532222
Email : sales-in@liferay.com

Contents

REGULAR FEATURES

Contents

COLUMNS

Buyers' Guide

DVD Of The Month

Editor
RAHUL CHOPRA

Editorial, Subscriptions & Advertising
DELHI (HQ)
D-87/1, Okhla Industrial Area, Phase I, New Delhi 110020
Ph: (011) 26810602, 26810603; Fax: 26817563
E-mail: info@efy.in

Missing Issues
E-mail: support@efy.in

BENGALURU
Ph: (080) 25260394, 25260023
E-mail: efyblr@efy.in

Customer Care
E-mail: support@efy.in

Back Issues
Kits 'n' Spares
New Delhi 110020
Ph: (011) 26371661, 26371662
E-mail: info@kitsnspares.com

Advertising
CHENNAI
Ph: (044) 42994363
E-mail: efyenq@efy.in

HYDERABAD
Ph: (040) 67172633
E-mail: efyenq@efy.in

KOLKATA
Ph: (033) 22294788
E-mail: efyenq@efy.in

MUMBAI
Ph: (022) 24950047, 24928520
E-mail: efymum@efy.in

PUNE
Ph: (020) 40147882
E-mail: efypune@efy.in

GUJARAT
Ph: (079) 61344948
E-mail: efyahd@efy.in

JAPAN
Tandem Inc., Ph: 81-3-3541-4166
E-mail: tandem@efy.in

SINGAPORE
Publicitas Singapore Pte Ltd
Ph: +65-6836 2272
E-mail: publicitas@efy.in

UNITED STATES
E & Tech Media
Ph: +1 860 536 6677
E-mail: veroniquelamarque@gmail.com

CHINA
Power Pioneer Group Inc.
Ph: (86 755) 83729797, (86) 13923802595
E-mail: powerpioneer@efy.in

TAIWAN
J.K. Media, Ph: 886-2-87726780 ext. 10
E-mail: jkmedia@efy.in

Exclusive News-stand Distributor (India)
IBH BOOKS AND MAGAZINES DISTRIBUTORS LTD
C/o Amar Chitra Katha Pvt. Ltd.,
Sumer Plaza, Marol Maroshi Road, Andheri (East),
Mumbai – 400 059
Ph: 022-49188888/9, 022-49188801
E-mail: info@ibhworld.com

SUBSCRIPTION RATES			
You Pay		Overseas	
Year	(₹)	(₹)	
Five	6000	3600	—
Three	3600	2520	—
One	1200	960	US$ 120

Kindly add ₹ 50/- for outside Delhi cheques.
Please send payments only in favour of **EFY Enterprises Pvt Ltd.**
Non-receipt of copies may be reported to support@efy.in—do mention your subscription number.

Zimbra Releases 8.5 Version
Collaboration
Anytime, Anywhere, Any Device

New Feature Highlights

■ Touch client for tablets and smartphones:

The secure, HTML5 mobile web application provides a device-specific user experience for Android and iOS devices. The Zimbra touch client can be tailored through open APIs and fully white labeled. It delivers anytime, anywhere mailbox access, through a unique Zimbra experience, that keeps people connected to their data.

■ Offline Web client:

Offline Web client support for Chrome and Firefox keeps Zimbra users connected, even when not taking advantage of native HTML5 data storage support. Users get the ability to work offline with access to one month's worth of data. And, IT administrators benefit from an offline client that doesn't increase the cost or management associated with a full desktop client.

■ Exchange Web Services:

The latest release adds new Exchange Web Services (EWS) support, enabling all mail, contacts, tasks and calendar functionality in Outlook for Mac. Administrators can add Outlook for Mac to the list of supported clients for BYOD environments, and users get to choose whatever Mac desktop client they prefer.

■ Zimbra Social integration:

Zimbra Collaboration 8.5 includes integrated support for Zimbra Social. Customers running both Zimbra products benefit from a shared user experience and single sign-on. Keeping employees connected to all of the collaboration touch points.

■ Document preview:

High fidelity document preview is now available, allowing users to preview documents in their Web browser.

Infrastructure Enhancements

■ Active-active:

Active-active is part of a multi-release effort to increase Zimbra Collaboration's scale and performance capabilities in complex Zimbra deployments. This encompasses a number of enhancements to the web application and server architecture, and introduces support for MariaDB. Zimbra Collaboration 9.x will continue this investment, helping eliminate downtime due to upgrades, maintenance or unplanned outages.

Feature Enhancements

■ Zimbra Connector for Microsoft Outlook (ZCO)

The Zimbra Connector for Microsoft Outlook (ZCO) provides real-time, two-way syncing of mail, contacts, tasks and calendars between Outlook and Zimbra. The latest release adds support for traditional Chinese and improvements for system administrators including: syncing, connection security and share message support. Administrators can better support and troubleshoot issues with logging improvements. Users can now accept shared mail folders and calendars from Outlook without opening the Zimbra Web client and will notice improved performance when syncing a large number of messages.

■ ActiveSync Performance and Scalability Enhancements

Service providers running large-scale ActiveSync deployments will benefit from decreased computing resource costs and increased user density per server. Administrators can now add BlackBerry 10 devices to the list of ActiveSync-enabled devices that are supported for BYOD environments. I'm very excited about what we are building at Zimbra and, with the addition of the Mezeo platform to the product portfolio, there will be some great product updates and advancements integrating sync and share into your daily work life, down the road.

Subscribing to *OSFY*

Here's saying 'Hi' to the *OSFY* team. I have always loved the content of your magazine, since the days when it was called *LFY*. However, I never subscribed to the magazine at any time, but would pick it up at libraries. Now, I want to subscribe for it. Also, from the Q&A section in your magazine, I have learnt that *OSFY* is available as an ezine too, which suits me. Can you please let me know how I can subscribe to just the ezine but not the paper version, as I am a little uncomfortable with collecting paper stuff.

—*Aditya*
aditya.btech@gmail.com

ED: Thank you for writing in to us and I'm glad to hear that you like our content. You can easily subscribe to OSFY by clicking on the following link:
http://ezines.efyindia.com/. Please get back to us in case of any other query or suggestion. We always value our readers' feedback.

A suggestion to start a series for Linux admins

First of all, hats off to the wonderful job you guys are doing at *OSFY*. I have been a reader of *OSFY* (earlier *LFY*) for the past four years. I have enjoyed each and every edition of the magazine. However, I would like to make a suggestion. Why don't you start a series on scripting, for Linux admins? I am sure it's a subject any Linux admin would be eager to learn about. Do consider starting a 'Learn Perl' series for Linux admins in coming editions of *OSFY* – maybe it could start with the basics and lead us on to advanced topics.

—*Jayakrishnan*
jayakrishnanlll@gmail.com

ED: Thanks for your appreciation. Such feedback really helps us to improve the quality of our content. We agree with you, that a series on scripting using Perl or Bash will be an interesting topic for sysadmins. We are already working with one of our regular authors on such a series. So expect to see articles on scripting soon. Feel free to get back to us for any other suggestions or feedback.

Getting an old issue of *OSFY*

I want to buy the May 2014 issue of *Open Source For You*. How can I get it now? I am from Pune. Please do help me.

—*Mujeeb Shaikh*
mujeeb.shaikh89@gmail.com

ED: Thanks for writing in to us. You can drop an email to support@efyindia.com or call us at 01126810601.

A request for Back Track Linux

Greetings to the *OSFY* team. I am a big fan of your magazine and also love the Linux distros that come with the DVD. I have one request. Could you provide Back Track Linux with the DVD since I have heard that it is a very powerful distro? Thanks in advance.

—*Parveen Kumar*
<parveen199214@gmail.com>

ED: We are pleased to know that you like the distros we feature on the DVD. Regarding Back Track, it is no longer being maintained. The updated version for penetration testing is now known as Kali Linux, which we bundled with the April 2014 issue of OSFY. This month, we are offering BackBox 4.0 with our magazine, which you will enjoy getting your hands on.

Writing for *OSFY*

I am a great admirer of open source software and projects, and *OSFY* has really helped me to get a clearer understanding about the innovations in this field. I eagerly look forward to each issue of your magazine. Recently, I came across Real Time Operating Systems and learnt about their importance. It would be great if you included some content on this topic in the magazine.

—*Athira Lekshmi*
athiralek@gmail.com

ED: We are glad that our content is useful to you and we value your feedback. We surely will include articles related to Real Time Operating Systems. You, too, are welcome to contribute content on the subject. Keep reading OSFY! END

Please send your comments or suggestions to:

The Editor,
Open Source For You,
D-87/1, Okhla Industrial Area, Phase I,
New Delhi 110020, **Phone:** 011-26810601/02/03,
Fax: 011-26817563, **Email:** osfyedit@efy.in

Android-based connected car stereo now available in India

Clarion, a Japanese manufacturer of car audio, navigation and communication systems, via its Asian arm Clarion Malaysia, has launched the Clarion AX1—an Android-based connected car stereo. The first-of-its-kind car stereo available in India, Clarion AX1 is a complete infotainment device, and promises a new and exciting experience for all gadget and technology enthusiasts. Clarion has introduced this Internet-ready device with the Android operating system and it is compatible with all smartphones. The device allows you to browse the Internet and also allows Wi-Fi connectivity. To up the entertainment quotient further, Clarion has tied up with T-series, which will give users unlimited access to a wide range of music albums and songs. Clarion's technology partner, Infogo, operates an online music store that offers a catalogue of more than 25 million fully licensed, DRM-free songs to choose from the world's biggest music labels. It has a 16.51 cm (6.5 inch) WVGA TFT LCD display with built-in navigation voice guidance.

Price: ₹ 55,990
Address: Supreme Audiotronics Pvt Ltd, A-62, Naraina Industrial Area Phase-1, New Delhi 110028; **Ph:** 011 4141 1778; **Website:** http://www.clariontechnologies.co.in/

Bose launches two great audio products

Bluetooth speakers: The SoundLink Color Bluetooth speaker has a completely new design but is still every inch a SoundLink. It weighs just 0.5 kg, and is 12.7 cm wide, 5.3 cm deep and 13.4 cm high to fit easily into a handbag, knapsack or the palm of your hand. Bose has combined exclusive dual-opposing passive radiators with two high-efficiency transducers for full-range sound, including deep, low-note performance. It connects wirelessly to a smartphone, tablet or any other Bluetooth-enabled device, and uses voice prompts available in several languages to simplify the set-up process, and identify which source is connected. Turn it off, and it remembers the last eight devices it was paired with, when powered back on. It then automatically connects to the two most recently used—your iPhone,

iPad, Android phone or other Bluetooth-enabled device. A 3.5 mm stereo auxiliary input is integrated on the back of the enclosure. The lithium-ion battery lasts up to eight hours of unplugged play time, and fully recharges with most USB power sources in as little as three hours. It comes in black, white, blue, red and mint.

Price: ₹ 11,138

Bluetooth headphones: The new SoundLink on-ear Bluetooth headphones deliver a new level of performance for this category. They offer crisp, powerful sound, new features and a design that's lighter and more comfortable than conventional Bluetooth headphones. Bose Active Equalisation and TriPort technology combine for smoother, more balanced sound. Mid-high frequencies are natural, and low-frequencies are detailed and full. Yet, there are no cords or cables, so you can take calls, or enjoy a video, movie or music, freely. These headphones debut new functionality and are so intuitive, anyone can use them. They connect up to two devices at a time and let you switch between each; so you can watch a video from your tablet while staying connected to your smartphone. Simple voice prompts identify who is calling, battery status and source connection. With commands on the ear-cup, users are in control: turn it on and off, answer and end a call, adjust volume, play/pause, or control tracks, without using your phone.

They feature soft ear cushions and a headband pad made of a fabric used in high-end automotive applications. They fold smoothly for compact storage in a matching case. The SoundLink Bluetooth headphones come in black or white, and charge easily with an included USB cable for up to 15 hours of listening.

Price: ₹ 21,038
Address: Bose Corporation India Private Limited, Salcon Aurum, 3rd Floor, Plot No 4, Jasola District Centre, New Delhi 110 025, India; **Ph:** +91 11 43080200; **Website:** www.boseindia.com

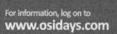

The smart LG G3 Stylus finally **debuts in India**

LG has launched the much-awaited LG G3 Stylus smartphone in India. The Stylus version of the G3 is a pen-enabled smartphone that inherits the core DNA of the acclaimed LG G3. The LG G3 Stylus, with its large display, stylus pen and LG's proprietary camera UX features, has a smartly-priced package to go with it. The proprietary Rubberdium stylus pen that slides inside the G3 Stylus feels comfortable in any hand and complements the phone's 13.97 cm large IPS display. Jotting and sketching are easier and more precise when paired with LG's QuickMemo+ which lets users take notes or draw directly on images or maps. The stylus is compatible with a number of third-party handwriting and drawing apps. Optimised for various 3G markets' wireless networks, the G3 Stylus will be offered with dual SIM devices with NFC capability in three colours— black, white and gold.

Price: ₹ 21,500

Address: LG Electronics, Plot No-51, Udyog Vihar, Surajpur Kasna Road, Greater Noida 201308; **Ph:** 0120-2560900; **Website:** www. in.lge.com

Samsung expands its iconic Note series with Galaxy Note 4

Samsung Electronics has launched the new Galaxy Note 4 in India. Blending an enhanced S Pen with a superior viewing experience, the Galaxy Note 4 supposedly provides users with a unique and powerful mobile experience in the market. It has an extraordinary 14.4 cm Quad HD (2560×1440 pixel) Super AMOLED display. The Galaxy Note 4 also sports an advanced camera.

The soft-textured back cover gives the device a luxurious finish while also providing a comfortable grip. The adaptive fast-charging feature in the Galaxy Note 4 charges the battery from 0 to 50 per cent in 33 minutes, which is 44 per cent faster than conventional charging.

Price: ₹ 58,300

Address: Samsung Electronics Pvt Ltd, Pinto Arcade, Opp Panjim Gymkhana, Campal, Panjim, Goa 403001; **Ph:** (91)-832-6641000; **Website:** www. samsungindiaestore.com

HP's new ProLiant Gen9 servers will help businesses to grow in India

HP has launched a new portfolio of HP ProLiant Generation 9 (Gen9) servers that will help customers reduce cost and complexity, accelerate IT service delivery and enable business growth. The new HP ProLiant Gen9 portfolio is a major delivery milestone in HP's compute strategy, which addresses IT demands with a vast pool of processing resources that can be located anywhere, scaled to any workload and available at all times. The servers are optimised for convergence, cloud and software-defined environments, and feature new technology innovations such as HP's unique PCIe accelerators and HP DDR4 SmartMemory that increase compute capacity and converged management across servers, storage and networking to enable a software defined enterprise.

Price: ₹ 1,73,255

Address: Hewlett Packard, No 66/2, Ward No 83, Bagmane Tech Park, Ground - 6th Floors, Wing A, 'Embassy Prime', CV Raman Nagar, Bengaluru 560093, Karnataka, India; **Ph:** 080 33841000; **Website:** http://www8.hp.com

Micromax launches Canvas A1, an Android One smartphone

With the arrival of a series of Android One smartphones, Micromax has also launched its Canvas A1 Android One smartphone, which is available in white and black. Micromax Canvas A1 supports a quad-core MediaTek processor, the Android 4.4.4 OS, a 5MP rear camera and a 2MP front shooter supported with a rechargeable lithium-ion 1700 mAh battery. It features an 11.43 cm FWVGA display with 1GB of RAM, 4GB internal storage and additional 35GB of free Google Drive storage.

Price: ₹ 6,499

Address: Micromax House, 90b, Gurgaon Sector-18, Gurgaon 122015, India; **Ph:** 911244811000; **Website:** http:// www.micromaxinfo.com

Shellshock—the latest threat to Linux and Mac OS X systems

The newly identified 'Shellshock' computer bug has already been exploited by hackers. A warning on this subject has been issued by researchers. 'Shellshock' is the first major Internet threat since the discovery of Heartbleed in April 2014, which affected OpenSSL encryption software. Several attacks took advantage of a long-existent but undiscovered vulnerability in the Linux and

Mac tool, Bash. With this malware, hackers trick Web servers into running any command that follows a carefully crafted series of characters in an http request. Thousands of machines can be attacked with this malware as it's

designed to make the machines part of a botnet of computers that easily come under the influence of hackers' commands. In at least one case, the attacked machines also launched distributed denial of service attacks that delivered a huge volume of junk traffic, as per security researchers.

Shellshock vulnerability exploits NAS devices: A recent report by FireEye reveals that the Shellshock vulnerability is spreading to NAS devices as well, which was first reported on September 24 of this year in the Bourne Again Shell (Bash). The report also states that the attackers are trying to exploit a code to hack into personal data. QNAP has pushed a security patch to fix it.

Attackers target Yahoo, Winzip and Lycos: According to the latest news from Yahoo, its servers were hacked by attackers from Romania. The company confirms that the Shellshock security hole was targeted by the attackers. Yahoo also said that there has been no loss of user data so far. Malicious scripts can be run on Bash if the Shellshock vulnerability is exploited. Since Bash runs commands on the system, hackers get direct access to the core system codes.

Red Hat and Apple release revised versions of patches against Shellshock: Mac, Linux and UNIX users can breathe a sigh of relief as the latest revisions of the bug fixes against Shellshock have been released by Apple and Red Hat. Apple has noted that a few Macs have been impacted by the bug and most users are already protected. The company had already promised that they will release an update shortly to address the issue. For older versions of OS X, there are separate downloads for Lion and Mountain Lion. The patch will be available through an OS X software update mechanism too.

GNOME 3.14 not to be part of Ubuntu 14.10

The GNOME 3.14 desktop will not be a part of Ubuntu 14.10, which is all set to be released on October 23 this year. If you have been wondering about this decision, then Ubuntu GNOME developer Ali Linx offered the following explanation in OMG! Ubuntu!: "Ubuntu, as all of you may know, has a strict schedule and something called 'feature freeze'." One of the most common

Red Hat breaks traditional storage barriers with open software-defined storage for multi-petabyte scale capacity

Red Hat has announced the availability of the newest major release of Red Hat Storage Server, an industry-leading open software-defined storage solution for scale-out file storage. The advanced capabilities in Red Hat Storage 3 are well-suited for data-intensive enterprise workloads including big data, operational analytics, and enterprise file sharing and collaboration. With its proven and validated workload solutions, Red Hat Storage Server 3 enables enterprises to curate enterprise data to increase responsiveness, control costs and improve operational efficiency. Red Hat is committed to building agile storage solutions through community-driven innovation to drive agility within the enterprise so as to better respond to competitive threats and changes in the evolving IT landscape. Based on the open source GlusterFS 3.6

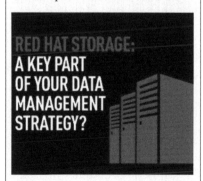

file system and Red Hat Enterprise Linux 6, Red Hat Storage Server 3 is designed to easily scale to support petabytes of data and offer granular control of your storage environment while lowering the overall cost of storage.

Opera Mini Web browser powers Samsung Gear S

Opera Mini has become the first Web browser on Samsung's Gear S, the Tizen-based wearable device platform. Users of this new smart watch will be able to enjoy Web browsing from their wrists, Opera Software has recently announced. With more than 250 million monthly users around the world, Opera Mini is known for its compression technology that shrinks the size of Web pages to sizes that are just 10 per cent their original. The result is a faster and more energy-efficient browsing experience. It helps to load image-heavy pages in a snap, with finger-friendly features for small-screen Web browsing. The Smart Page gives users all their social updates and the latest news on one screen. Opera Mini's speed dial features website shortcuts as large buttons, enabling Gear S users to reach their favourite sites in a single tap. Private browsing removes any trace of the Web pages visited on the device.

SUSE and MariaDB expand Linux ecosystem on IBM POWER8

SUSE and MariaDB Corporation (formerly SkySQL) have announced a partnership that expands the Linux application ecosystem on IBM Power systems. As a result, customers can now run a wider variety of applications on POWER8, increasing their flexibility and choice while working within their existing IT infrastructure. The partnership was unveiled at IBM Enterprise 2014, supporting the US$ 1 billion investment to be spent over the next five years to develop Linux and open source technologies on IBM Power systems. This is the first of several partnerships to be announced by SUSE with the upcoming release of SUSE Linux Enterprise 12–the latest version of the most interoperable platform for mission-critical computing across physical, virtual and cloud environments. MariaDB Enterprise will be optimised for SUSE Linux Enterprise Server 12 on IBM POWER8-based servers.

CALENDAR OF FORTHCOMING EVENTS

Name, Date and Venue	Description	Contact Details and Website
Open Source India, November 7-8, 2014; NIMHANS Center, Bengaluru	Asia's premier open source conference that aims to nurture and promote the open source ecosystem across the sub-continent.	Omar Farooq; Email: omar.farooq@efy.in; Ph: 09958881862 http://www.osidays.com
CeBit November 12-14, 2014; BIEC, Bengaluru	This is one of the world's leading business IT events, and offers a combination of services and benefits that will strengthen the Indian IT and ITES markets.	Website: http://www.cebit-india.com/
5th Annual Datacenter Dynamics Converged; December 9, 2014; Riyadh	The event aims to assist the community in the datacentre domain by exchanging ideas, accessing market knowledge and launching new initiatives.	Praveen Nair; Email: Praveen.nair@datacenterdynamics.com; Ph: +91 9820003158; Website: http://www.datacenterdynamics.com/
Hostingconindia December 12-13, 2014; NCPA, Jamshedji Bhabha Theatre, Mumbai	This event will be attended by Web hosting companies, Web design companies, domain and hosting resellers, ISPs and SMBs from across the world.	Website: http://www.hostingcon.com/contact-us/

issues with Ubuntu GNOME has been that the distro doesn't integrate the new packages that are released as things are not as simple as they seem. Ubuntu GNOME is very much an official flavour of the Ubuntu ecosystem and the developers need to follow a strict release schedule. One of the most important steps is 'feature freeze'. This is a point in the cycle where all the new features and major modifications for the system stop and the developers focus on bug fixes only.

Here comes the Linux 3.17 kernel and it fixes the UNIX 2038 bug

Linus Torvalds has kept the 'Shuffling Zombie Juror' code name for Linux 3.17, which finally got released with lots of great features and is being considered

a big improvement by experts. Hence, Linux 3.17 must be called a very exciting update and for any avid Steam user, this release allows controllers to get connected to desktops via Microsoft Xbox One controller support, without any vibration. In addition, the open source NVIDIA driver has also received several improvements. Distros like Arch, Fedora, Korora and Manjaro, which are open to frequent updates, are expected to get the Linux 3.17 update soon. The release fixes the UNIX 2038 bug, which was slated to impact Linux systems after 24 years (in 2038), much like the worries related to Y2K (in year 2000 -- a flaw that was only fixed on many systems in 1999). Linux 3.17 contains only this one patch to fix the UNIX 2038. The addition of memory fences is certainly an important feature in Linux 3.17. Linux kernel developer, David Herrmann has sent out mailing lists that explain

OSFYClassifieds

Classifieds for Linux & Open Source IT Training Institutes

WESTERN REGION

Linux Lab (empowering linux mastery)
Courses Offered: Enterprise Linux
& VMware

Address (HQ): 1104, D' Gold House,
Nr. Bharat Petrol Pump, Ghyaneshwer
Paduka Chowk, FC Road, Shivajinagar
Pune-411 005
Contact Person: Mr.Bhavesh M. Nayani
Contact No.: +020 60602277,
+91 8793342945
Email: info@linuxlab.org.in
Branch(es): coming soon
Website: www.linuxlab.org.in

Linux Training & Certification
Courses Offered: RHCSA,
RHCE, RHCVA, RHCSS,
NCLA, NCLP, Linux Basics,
Shell Scripting,
(Coming soon) MySQL

Address (HQ): 104B Instant Plaza,
Behind Nagrik Stores,
Near Ashok Cinema,
Thane Station West - 400601,
Maharashtra, India
Contact Person: Ms. Swati Farde
Contact No.: +91-22-25379116/
+91-9869502832
Email: mail@ltcert.com
Website: www.ltcert.com

NORTHERN REGION

GRRAS Linux Training and Development Center

Courses Offered: RHCE, RHCSS, RHCVA,
CCNA, PHP, Shell Scripting (online training
is also available)

Address (HQ): GRRAS Linux Training and
Development Center, 219, Himmat Nagar,
Behind Kiran Sweets, Gopalpura Turn,
Tonk Road, Jaipur, Rajasthan, India
Contact Person: Mr. Akhilesh Jain
Contact No.: +91-141-3136868 /
+91-9983340133, 9785598711, 9887789124
Email: info@grras.com
Branch(es): Nagpur, Pune
Website(s): www.grras.org, www.grras.com

SOUTHERN REGION

*astTECS Academy
Courses Offered: Basic Asterisk Course,
Advanced Asterisk Course, Free PBX
Course, Vici Dial Administration Course

Address (HQ): 1176, 12th B Main,
HAL 2nd Stage, Indiranagar,
Bangalore - 560008, India
Contact Person: Lt. Col. Shaju N. T.
Contact No.: +91-9611192237
Email: info@asterisk-training.com
Website: www.asttecs.com,
www.asterisk-training.com

Advantage Pro
Courses Offered: RHCSS, RHCVA,
RHCE, PHP, Perl, Python, Ruby, Ajax,
A prominent player in Open Source
Technology

Address (HQ): 1 & 2 , 4th Floor,
Jhaver Plaza, 1A Nungambakkam
High Road, Chennai - 600 034, India
Contact Person: Ms. Rema
Contact No.: +91-9840982185
Email: enquiry@vectratech.in
Website(s): www.vectratech.in

Duestor Technologies

Courses Offered: Solaris, AIX,
RHEL, HP UX, SAN Administration
(Netapp, EMC, HDS, HP),
Virtualisation(VMWare, Citrix, OVM),
Cloud Computing, Enterprise
Middleware.

Address (H.Q.): 2-88, 1st floor,
Sai Nagar Colony, Chaitanyapuri,
Hyderabad - 060
Contact Person: Mr. Amit
Contact Number(s): +91-9030450039,
+91-9030450397.
E-mail id(s): info@duestor.com
Websit(es): www.duestor.com

IPSR Solutions Ltd.

Courses Offered: RHCE, RHCVA,
RHCSS, RHCDS, RHCA,
Produced Highest number of
Red Hat professionals
in the world

Address (HQ): Merchant's
Association Building, M.L. Road,
Kottayam - 686001,
Kerala, India
Contact Person: Benila Mendus
Contact No.: +91-9447294635
Email: training@ipsrsolutions.com
Branch(es): Kochi, Kozhikode,
Thrissur, Trivandrum
Website: www.ipsr.org

Linux Learning Centre
Courses Offered: Linux OS Admin
& Security Courses for Migration,
Courses for Developers, RHCE,
RHCVA, RHCSS, NCLP

Address (HQ): 635, 6th Main Road,
Hanumanthnagar,
Bangalore - 560 019, India
Contact Person: Mr. Ramesh Kumar
Contact No.: +91-80-22428538,
26780762, 65680048 /
+91-9845057731, 9449857731
Email: info@linuxlearningcentre.com
Branch(es): Bangalore
Website: www.linuxlearningcentre.com

Eastern Region

**Academy of Engineering and
Management (AEM)**
Courses Offered: RHCE, RHCVA,
RHCSS,Clustering & Storage,
Advanced Linux, Shell
Scripting, CCNA, MCITP, A+, N+

Address (HQ): North Kolkata, 2/80
Dumdum Road, Near Dumdum
Metro Station, 1st & 2nd Floor,
Kolkata - 700074
Contact Person: Mr. Tuhin Sinha
Contact No.: +91-9830075018,
9830051236
Email: sinhatuhin1@gmail.com
Branch(es): North & South Kolkata
Website: www.aemk.org

Linux Foundation launches the Dronecode Project

The Linux Foundation has launched a project that will develop open source software to enable non-military unmanned aerial vehicles (UAVs), popularly known as drones. Called the Dronecode Project, it was launched on October 13 at the Linux Conference in Dusseldorf, Germany. With this project, a new member has been added to the Foundation's Collaboration Projects initiative, which brings together best practices in technology to develop open source codes.

The Dronecode Project will also join the Yocto Project in order to build embedded Linux platforms. The project is based on APM UAV software and code, which are hosted by the project's co-founding member, 3D Robotics. Other founding members are Box, DroneDeploy and jDrones. Dronecode will help in data analysis, storage and in the displays for drones.

Drones are quite commonly used nowadays, courtesy the unending automated wars in Iraq, Pakistan and Afghanistan. The project will be headed by rsync author and Samba co-lead Andrew Tridgell, who is also the lead maintainer in the development of APM. Executive director of the Linux Foundation, Jim Zemlin told eWEEK, that potential synergies are present between Dronecode and the Yocto Project. Along with the APM UAV application code, the Dronecode Project also includes the PX4 project code. Zemlin is pretty confident about the Dronecode Project.

the security improvements in Linux 3.17. The new release includes file sealing protection.

Another German city abandons Windows to adopt Linux at its administrative offices

Germany is known for being an early adopter of open source software. Munich city completely adopted open source technology quite a while ago. And now, government offices in the city of Gummersbach have reportedly switched to open source technology. Gummersbach is a small city compared to Munich, with a population of barely 50,000. The administration considered switching to open source technology in 2007

and started the migration process back then. Over 300 PCs in the administrative offices of Gummersbach have adopted the SUSE Linux operating system. The city's representative confirmed that Linux has replaced the Windows XP OS on these PCs. The official announcement of this migration has been published on the European Commission's website. It will take a long time to replace Windows entirely, but it's a good initiative. We might see more cities in Germany soon follow suit. There is no doubt that this action will increase the popularity of Linux in Germany amongst citizens also.

Demand for Linux Foundation certification increases!

According to a recent study, the demand for Linux jobs continues to increase. According to a recent report by Dice, 93 per cent of employers are looking to hire Linux professionals. The best way to increase the probability of getting a Linux job is to clear the Linux Foundation's certification exams. As of now, Linux Foundation (LF) has two attractive certification programmes - Certified SysAdmin (LFCS) and Certified Engineer (LFCE). Linux Foundation's certification exams are one level higher than the Linux

Professional Institute (LPI) certifications. The former are designed to be as high level as Red Hat Certified System Administrator (RHCSA) and are not easy to pass. The success rate of these exams is below 60 per cent but they are highly recommended by those who have already taken them. The exams are held from a Linux shell. There are online guides that help you succeed in LF certification exams. A free preparation guide is available on Linux Foundation's website as well.

Red Hat Enterprise Linux 6.6 released

Red Hat, a provider of open source solutions, has released the latest version of the Red Hat Enterprise Linux 6 (RHEL) platform, version 6.6. Users of the newer RHEL 7 will also be allowed to run RHEL 6 apps in a container. RHEL 6 was launched in 2010, and the latest release offers a stable and secure foundation, enabling organisations to build infrastructure according to business requirements through better flexibility. In June this year, Red Hat had launched

RHEL 7. In RHEL 6.6, support will be provided to enable a cross-realm Kerberos, through an RHEL 7 server. RHEL 6.6 will also benefit from Red Hat's 'Performance Co-Pilot' feature, which was initially introduced in RHEL 7. According to Steve Almy, the product manager for Red Hat's Platform Business Unit, Red Hat customers will now be able to monitor performance across RHEL 6 and 7 servers in a consistent manner. RHEL 6.6 will also benefit from performance improvements. Red Hat will be providing a supported container feature in RHEL 7 enabling RHEL 6 applications to run without any changes.

CyanogenMod 11.0 M11 released for supported devices

The CyanogenMod team recently announced the release of CM 11.0 M11, which has been rolled out for supported devices.
The company has provided the complete change log at its blog post. The M11 builds are now available for CM-users via the CM updater app on Android devices, over-the-air (OTA). Users can even install it manually from the CM Downloads website. Since the builds are still under the release process, it might take some time for a specific build, based on the device model, to appear. As far as Android 4.4.4 is concerned, CyanogenMod 11.0 M11 has been successfully released for more than 80 Android devices and their variants.

SUSECon 2014 to highlight advances in enterprise Linux, the cloud and in storage technologies

SUSE has announced the sponsors, as well as the keynote and breakout session details for its upcoming SUSECon 2014 global technical conference, in November 17-21 at Orlando, Florida. SUSECon is an energetic and interactive platform for information exchange among customers, partners and open source enthusiasts. The conference, aimed at enterprise IT users, will include keynote and technical sessions, technology showcases, and opportunities to interact with business leaders, analysts, technical experts, as well as other users and solutions providers.

This year's content will highlight the
latest technical advances in enterprise Linux, OpenStack cloud, Ceph storage and other open source technologies, as well as reveal the future direction of SUSE apart from unique industry insights. Michael Miller, SUSE vice president of global alliances and marketing, will host the event. Keynote guests will include James Staten, vice president and principal analyst of infrastructure and operations at Forrester Research, and Nils Brauckmann, president and general manager of SUSE. There will also be plenty of interviews with customers and sponsors. SUSECon breakout sessions will feature compelling technical content presented by SUSE engineers and product managers, SUSE customers and partners, and community enthusiasts. A full session catalogue is now available. The wide range of sessions will address new and existing technologies, customer scenarios and deployments, and how-tos for the implementation of Linux and cloud technologies.

The Best Features of Google's Android 5.0 Lollipop

Since the preview, Google has added lots of new features to the final release of the latest Android version. Let's take a look at the top 10 features of the much-awaited Android 5.0 Lollipop.

Back in June, Google previewed and teased us with Android L at the Google I/O developer event and ever since then, the final version has been awaited with much eagerness. Finally, on October 15, Android 5.0 Lollipop was launched on devices like Nexus 6, Nexus 9 and Nexus Player. Since the preview, Google has added lots of new features to the final release of this new Android version. Let's look at its top 10 features.

1. Material Design: a new design language

Google's last design language was Holo, which was replaced by Material Design, which has been used in Android L. Google has been continuously updating its design guidelines for developers to start making Material Design apps. With Lollipop, Google is focusing on the main thing – Android's consistency across all devices. Android Lollipop will be omnipresent across phones, tablets, watches, cars and TVs too. Lollipop will have a flat look for its UI and all icons. The Material Design means menus

will respond more promptly. So Android Lollipop is all about a consistent design experience across all Android devices and with this design, elements can dynamically shrink and expand. Most importantly, the interface has a 3D appearance overall.

2. Battery life fixes

Google has added a new battery saver feature to the latest Android version, which claims to extend the battery life of devices up to 90 minutes. This Android version will display the estimated time left to fully charge the device when plugged in and also the time left before the user needs to recharge the device. Android phones have always suffered from battery life issues due to apps and services running in the background. The power-saving mode has been missing from older versions of Android. You'll be able to restrict syncing, background data and also screen brightness to extend battery life. The power-saving mode has been tuned in a better way to the Android 5.0

Lollipop. The battery use menu has got a better graph, which informs users which apps are draining the battery. More battery life is always welcome so Android Lollipop is a winner for millions of Android users across the globe.

3. Notification settings

Android 5.0 Lollipop has lock-screen displays and rich notification settings. Users can view and respond to messages directly from the locked screen, and the richer notification settings in the new Android version include floating descriptive notifications on the top of activities. These notifications can be viewed or dismissed without moving away from any activity. On Android Lollipop, Google has offered better control over notifications. Users can control notifications from apps and sensitive content can be kept hidden. The 'Priority mode' can also be turned on via the volume button of the device. There is one more feature called the'Do Not Disturb' mode, just like in Apple's iOS, which allows users to selectively silence notifications and calls. The entire look and feel of the notifications is changing as lock-screen can be easily accessed now, along with a revamped pull-down menu. The layout and location of the notifications have been completely changed and lock-screen widgets have been removed from Android 5.0.

4. Security enhancements

Android 5.0 will allow encryption, by default. You can encrypt your Android device even now, but it's a painstaking job. You need to plug in your phone and the encryption process takes a minimum of 30 minutes. And just to warn you, if anything goes wrong, your data will be lost. But with Android 5.0, encryption will be automatic. Android 5.0 features an opt-in kill-switch known as 'Factory Reset Protection' which allows users to wipe out the device's data, if they wish to. With this Android version, you can also unlock your phone in an easier way without entering a PIN or drawing the pattern. You can use an Android watch to unlock your phone, which is kept in close proximity. Lollipop also comes with SELinux enforcement, which means better protection against viruses and malware.

5. New quick settings

Google wants to curb swipes on devices that are needed to access important functions like Wi-Fi, Bluetooth and GPS activation. The new Android includes built-in tools for the flashlight, hotspot and screen cast controls, which means you can get rid of many third party apps now. Setting up an Android device will become faster with Android 5.0, as the new device can be set up just by tapping it on the old device, though this requires NFC support. All apps from Google Play will be transferred to the new device, if the same Google account is used. In certain situations, you can also adjust brightness, manually.

6. A new messenger app

There is a new messenger app in Android 5.0, which comes with Nexus 6 and is said to be a simplified version of Google Hangouts. This messenger has been designed for sending and receiving SMS and MMS messages on Android in a quicker and easier way. More updates about this messenger are still awaited though.

7. Performance boosts

Android 5.0 supports 64-bit and the new Nexus 9 also features a 64-bit chip, though Nexus 6 doesn't. Well, this kind of performance boost will not make a very huge difference for average users but Google will be shipping native 64-bit versions of Gmail, Maps and other apps too. But this development will not mean much if you are using a 32-bit device. The runtime environment in the new Android version is ART, which promises four times better performance and better desktop level graphics performance too.

8. An updated camera

The updated camera settings support advanced features like burst mode and fine-settings tuning. Full resolution frames around 30fps can be captured in this new update and shooting can be done in raw formats like YUV and Bayer RAW. Android 5.0 also supports UHD 4K video playback, tunnelled video for high quality video playback on Android TV and improved live streaming. Professional features have also been added like controlling settings for the sensor, lens and a flash, per individual frame. In Android 5.0, developers will be able to implement their own technology to take full advantage of hardware and any mediocre camera can be transformed to a better one.

9. Device sharing

Device sharing features have been integrated in Android 5.0, which allow users to share their device with family members and friends without giving access to sensitive content. It features a guest user mode with custom options for access, which allows users to fix the place of the screen that is displayed. There is also a feature in Lollipop that allows users to log in to another Android phone to access synced messages and content, if the device is forgotten at home.

10. Other updates

There are some more features in this OS besides other fixes and improvements. In this new OS, finding things will become easier with improved search indexing, and search results will be saved across different apps and devices.

Other relevant features of Android 5.0 include improved hardware keyboard accessory support, support for 15 new languages including Bengali, Kannada, Malayalam, Marathi, Tamil and Telugu, improved audio and video capabilities, and improved Internet connectivity with more powerful Bluetooth low energy capabilities. END

By: Sanchari Banerjee

The author is a member of the editorial team, who loves to explore innovations in the technology world.

Network Switches—An Absolute Necessity for Networking

This buying guide on network switches, which are also called Ethernet switches, will help SMEs and companies in the SOHO segment to design, configure and build their networks with ease.

Popularly known as a switching hub, a network switch is a computer networking device, which connects devices together by using a form of packet switching. It is one asset that's essential for designing, configuring and building your networks. It is a device that lets you connect more Ethernet-based devices to your network without causing any confusion or chaos. It makes your life easy, as each device connected to the network switch can automatically communicate with the other devices already connected to the switch. So before buying a network switch, read on!

Who needs a network/Ethernet switch?

You might be confused about whether or not you need a network switch. You certainly do not require a network switch if you have just one computer to work on, if your Internet usage is limited, and if your computer is directly attached to your ADSL modem. A network switch may not be needed at homes but it is a must in offices or organisations as networking plays a vital role in building network infrastructure.

You need a network switch to build the network's infrastructure. Switches used in such networks are of two types: wired or wireless. Though a lot of people use wireless switches, wired switches are still in high demand and preferred by many. You definitely need a wired network if your wireless connection is low on bandwidth, especially when you are transferring heavy files, want to back up your Mac, your kids want to play online games or download movies, and your spouse wants to stream music—all at the same time, without your network breaking down. For all this, you need an Ethernet network switch.

Factors to keep in mind while selecting a network switch

When you are considering buying a network switch, there are a few factors to be kept in mind. If you want to scale your network in the near future, go for a larger number of ports. Careful planning prior to the purchase will save you money and time, apart from ensuring that you do not end up buying a switch which doesn't suit your requirements. Here are some important factors that should determine the device you select.

1. **Number of users:** Consider the number of users that you want your network to support. If you only have four or five devices that you need to connect, then an 8-port switch should be enough for your needs. This is how you also end up saving the money and space.

2. **Basic network infrastructure:** For a small network of up to 50 users, one switch should be enough; whereas, if you want your switch to support more users, you might have to go for multiple switches.

3. **Determine the role of the switch:** If you plan to build a large network, you should have one or more switches acting as a 'core'. These switches should be fast and able to handle the traffic load. Generally, a Gigabit switch works well as a core switch and access switches (where individual users connect) are likely to be slower than a core switch. If you require to connect a few computers (four or five), a single access switch is what you need.

4. **Network requirements:** You need to determine your network requirements—do your users need a fast network but with a low latency, or do they require to transfer larger volumes of data? In the latter case, a switch supporting Gigabit Ethernet might be appropriate. Whereas, if the network is used more for Internet and network resource access then a 100 megabit port should be sufficient for your requirements. Figure out how many edge Power over Ethernet (PoE) and PoE+ ports you require and at what speed. Besides, the number of both edge/primary and uplink types and ports are important factors.

5. **Choosing a vendor:** You may not buy a network switch directly from the manufacturer and may prefer one brand over another. There are quite a few companies offering network switches with different specifications, some of whom are mentioned later in the article. Figuring this out requires some research before you get to know which brand best suits your requirements. Make sure that the company is giving you all the possible support like a 24×7 helpline, hardware replacement, repairs, etc.

6. **Look for different features:** Most switches are not restricted to having just two or three features, but offer many, which can be considered once your usage and requirements are decided upon. The different options include wired or wireless switches, managed or unmanaged devices, 3-layer capability, etc. These features need to be considered if the switch is being bought for offices, organisations or larger enterprise networks.

7. **Price vs features:** For a lot of people, price is more important than the features a product offers. But sometimes, considering features over price makes more sense. There are many brands in the market which offer

affordable, lower-end switches for homes and small enterprises. These work pretty well in a small network, but they often lack several features that you might need, which are available only in the expensive models. A few companies offer moderately priced switches but again, their products would not have features which an high-end switch would offer. And the most expensive switches are usually difficult to configure. Considering all these issues, the best thing one can do is to keep the specifications and budget in mind when researching the product.

Some of the best projectors available in the Indian market

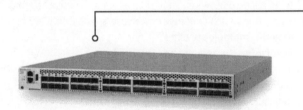

Brocade 6510

The Brocade 6510 is a 48-port, high-performance, enterprise-class switch that meets the demands of highly virtualised and private cloud storage environments by delivering market-leading Gen 5 fibre channel technology.

- **Form factor:** 1 U
- **Dimensions (W×H×D):** 43.7×4.3×44.3 cm
- **Throughput:** 128GBps
- **Number of ports:** 48
- **Speed:** 10/100/1000 Mbps

Juniper EX2200

A carrier-class architecture, coupled with the Junos OS, enables Juniper's field-proven EX Series of switches to provide carrier-class reliability for every application.

- **Form factor:** Fixed platform, virtual chassis configuration consisting of up to four switches
- **Dimensions (W×H×D):** 44.1×4.4×25.4 cm
- **Throughput: 24P/24T:** 42 Mbps (wire speed)

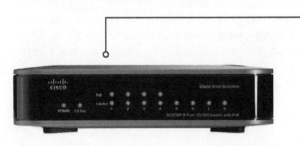

Cisco SD208P

The Cisco SD208P 8-port 10/100 switch offers the performance and ease-of-use you need to get your business connected quickly and easily. Designed and priced for small businesses that want a simple network solution, the switch works right out-of-the-box with no software to configure, and features PoE to power network attached devices.

- **Ports:** RJ-45 10/100
- **Dimensions (W×H×D):** 14×3.3×14 cm

D Link DES-1005A

The DES-1005A 5-port 10/100 switch allows you to quickly set up a fast, reliable and efficient wired network in your home or office. Powerful, yet easy to use, this device allows users to simply plug any port to either a 10MBps or 100Mbps network to multiply bandwidth, boost response time and satisfy heavy load demands.

- **Dimensions (W×H×D):** 190×120×38 mm
- **Ports:** 5-port 10/100BASE-T

By: Manvi Saxena

The author is a part of the editorial team at EFY.

Open Source India 2014-11th Edition: A FOSS Event You Just Can't Miss!

Open Source India is one of Asia's biggest conventions on open source. This year, the conference-cum-expo is being held at the NIMHANS Convention Centre in Bengaluru on November 7-8. Apart from various networking sessions and workshops, the event will host a number of tracks that will keep you updated on all that is happening in the world of FOSS.

Formerly known as LinuxAsia, Open Source India (OSI) is an industry-cum-community event where FOSS lovers and open source enthusiasts come together to share, discuss and spread knowledge on open source technologies. The event brings together stalwarts from the tech industry, not just to spread awareness and knowledge related to open source but also to share their success stories with those attending the event. The event aims to bring together IT implementers, IT developers and budding tech professionals on a single platform. Balaji Keshav Raj, director, platform strategy and marketing, Microsoft Corporation, India, who has been associated with OSI since a long time, shares his view about this event: "We have been associated with OSI as we like to interact with IT developers and implementers. Also, through this conference, we share how Microsoft handles work beautifully on the cloud platform. I am constantly in touch with the organisers of OSI, and they are doing a great job!"

Highlights of OSI 2013

1. *2600 registrations:* Open Source India 2013 was jampacked! There was an unmistakable buzz in the air as the registrations for the event crossed 2600. This is what makes Open Source India one of Asia's biggest open source conferences.

2. *64 eminent speakers:* There were more than 64 speakers who shared their valuable knowledge on the latest open source tools and also showcased what was best about the companies they worked for. These eminent personalities included stalwarts like Dr K Y Srinivasan, principal architect, Microsoft; Jacob Singh, regional director,

Tracks @ OSI 2014

Day 1 (November 7, 2014)

FOSS For Everyone (Pass Required: Silver)
- A half-day track with multiple sessions on how FOSS can be used.
- Target audience: Everyone interested in free and open source software/solutions

Cloud (Pass Required: Silver)
- A half-day track with multiple sessions on: how to choose the best cloud solution and the latest developments in cloud solutions.
- Target audience: CXOs, IT heads, IT managers, IT implementers and cloud developers

Mobile App Development (Pass Required: Gold)
- A full-day track with multiple sessions on what's hot on the mobile development front.
- Target audience: Software developers (mobile/Web)

OpenStack Mini Conf (Pass Required: Silver)
- A half-day track where you can meet the people who have the expertise in OpenStack.
- Target audience: Anybody interested in Cloud and OpenStack

Kernel Dev Day (Pass Required: Gold)
- This track is specially for the people interested in knowing more about kernel development. The talks will be on the latest developments in the Linux kernel and its impact on modern devices.
- Target audience: Kernel developers and device driver developers

Day 2 (November 8, 2014)

Web App Development (Pass Required: Gold)
- A half-day track with multiple sessions on Web development. Attend to know more about the latest in Web development using open source.
- Target audience: Web developers

IT Infrastructure (Pass Required: Silver)
- A half-day track where you can meet the experts on CloudStack.
- Target audience: CXOs, IT heads, IT managers, IT implementers

Database Day (Pass Required: Gold)
- Open source databases have always been of great importance. This is a full-day track highlighting different aspects of these databases.
- Target audience: Project managers, developers, IT implementers, DBAs

Success Stories (Pass Required: Silver)
- Open source has helped many organisations save a lot of money. People who have benefited with the use of open source will share their success stories in this track.
- Target audience: Project managers, IT implementers/admins, CTOs, CIOs

For more information, visit our website www.osidays.com

Speakers @ OSI 2013 share their experiences with us

Lux Rao

CTO, Technology
Services, HP India

Association with OSI...
OSI is the largest open source forum in the country, and it brings in a lot of open source enthusiasts on one common platform. That's a compelling reason for all the vendors, developers and organisations associated with open source in some way to come and share their knowledge and expertise.

Experiences at OSI 2013...
It gets better every year. I would say that OSI has exceptional content. It values the speakers and that is why I think people want to come back to it.

Why OSI..
To put it in simple words, people should attend OSI, as they can be a part of the world developing around open source and can get to know the latest from leading experts. The event also offers tremendous potential for networking, where delegates can interact with user groups and discuss challenges, skills, techniques and why it's important to adopt open source. I look forward to OSI 2014.

Association with OSI...
I associate with OSI because it is one of the best open source conferences and I like the focus of this event. We have not just been a part of OSI but we constantly keep contributing to the magazine. We look forward to continuing our association with OSI as well as OSFY!

Experiences at OSI 2013...
The theme and agenda was good, and that's why we expected the turnout to be more. The event itself was organised and presented well.

Why OSI..
We do not have a very good open source conference in India. OSI represents emerging trends as the conference's theme, and the best thing about this event is that it does not have a static focus—it changes with the dynamic needs of what people are looking for in a conference like this. I look forward to this event.

Vidya Sakar

Engineering
Manager, Dell

Vikas Jha

Director, Open Source
Technology, Unotech Pvt Ltd

Association with OSI...
OSI is a wonderful platform for all the people and organisations who have implemented open source. It is our pleasure to be associated with OSI.

Experiences at OSI 2013...
I had a great time sharing my knowledge and experiences. I would want OSI to organise more networking sessions. The themes, workshops and tracks were smartly placed!

Why OSI..
OSI, because it's India's only open source conference and that, too, at such an advanced level. It is quite helpful to all the tech buffs who want to implement open source in their ventures. I will definitely be a part of OSI 2014.

Association with OSI...
Open Source India is one of the largest events based on open source. It offers the latest buzz and happenings related to FOSS. I get the opportunity to share my inputs on implementing open source.

Experiences at OSI 2013...
It is always a pleasure to be a part of knowledgeable conferences and especially at OSI, as it is a platform where the open source community comes together.

Why OSI...
Like I mentioned, OSI is one of the largest events based on open source and it gives me great pleasure to be a part of it. I have higher expectations from OSI 2014 and I look forward to it.

Rajiv Papneja

Chief Operations
Officer, ESDS

Speakers @ OSI 2014 share their plans for the event

Jacob Singh Regional Director, Acquia India

Being one of the most recognised open source companies, it is important that we come and extend support to you and contribute to the ecosystem. It is also an opportunity to interact with the people in the same field, learn from them, build new relations and try to make money out of open source. This time we plan to talk about personalisation, customising content on websites depending upon the visitors, and a lot more! I think the event last time was a little dry in terms of the business audience. And I think I would want to get rid of the 'gold', 'platinum' criteria for passes. Regarding the rest, the event is always a treat!

Dibya Prakash Consultant, ECDzone

I have been associated with OSI since the event was called LinuxAsia, and one of the major reasons for this is that it is a combination of technology and business. It drives business and technology together. We plan to speak on mobility, and we also have plans to conduct a workshop on mobile development. We are going to deliver a talk/ session on mobile testing and the job opportunities in this space. This event has been growing pretty well.

Prajod Vettiyattil Architect, Wipro Technologies

I have been working with the open source division of Wipro for four years, and I have been a speaker at OSI in 2011. The reason for my association is the wide variety of interesting tracks, the dedicated audience and the networking possibilities. Open source is a very big ocean and events like these are always a treat to attend. I plan to speak on Big Data, Hadoop and ApacheSpark. I am looking forward to this event.

Mubeen Jukaku Technical Head, Emertxe

Ours is a company based on open source software and we operate in that domain. OSI, being the largest conference on open source, brings us here. We are passionate about contributing our content to this conference as there will be IT implementers, developers, etc. This event will give us an opportunity to share our experiences among the attendees. We have planned to speak on Linux device drivers.

Piyush Mathur Senior Solutions Advisor, Zimbra

We have been associated with Open Source India, as Zimbra is an open source-based company. Our primary expectations from this event are a lot of coverage and to get some leads. Ours is a product company and we have three open source-based products to sell in the market. Among other topics, we are speaking on the Zimbra collaboration.

Zimbra is an open source product. At this event, we expect customers and prospects who are interested in open source technology, and who evangelise open source as a technology. We are sure we will find the right set of people in this event.

Acquia India; Lux Rao, CTO, technology services, HP India; Vidya Sakar, engineering manager, Dell, India; and Vikas Jha, director, Unotech Pvt Ltd.

3. *A new track called 'Success stories' was introduced:* In the 10th edition of OSI, we introduced a new track, called 'Success stories'. Here, CIOs and IT implementers of companies narrated their stories on how open source technology helped them leverage their IT infrastructure and enhance their ROI. This track is of immense use to those who want to maximise their business' productivity through open source.

4. *Technical workshops:* There were more than 10 technical workshops at OSI 2013. These included: Android application development, building your personal cloud with OpenStack, developing games with HTML5 for the Web and the mobile, Android application testing for consumer and enterprise applications, to name a few.

What OSI 2014 offers you

Every year, OSI becomes bigger and better. The 11th edition of OSI aims to take this event a notch higher by focusing on the open source ecosystem in Asia, and more specifically, in India. If you are a developer, IT implementer, CIO, CTO or just someone who is passionate about open source, you will find information-packed sessions and great content related to FOSS. If you are not a FOSS enthusiast but curious to know what it is all about, this event is for you as well. Of the many interesting tracks, eminent speakers and technical workshops, there are bound to be some amazing features that will definitely entice you to the event.

- *Wipro will be hiring at this event:* IT giant, Wipro Technologies, has tied up with Open Source India 2014 for recruiting applicants for diverse profiles. For more information on this, visit *www.osidays.com*
- *HP Helion's developer challenge:* HP is conducting a developer challenge at the event for all the attendees. Not much information has been shared by the company as yet, but it surely will be worth the wait!
- *Microsoft's interoperability demonstrations:* Microsoft is arranging a special hands-on event on how it interoperates with open source software. It is a not-to-be-missed workshop!

Be a part of OSI, and celebrate the spirit of FOSS!

We have given you enough reasons to be a part of this tremendous event. If that is not sufficient, we have more to offer. Come to the event and build networks because we offer networking sessions as well. The Q&A sessions in each track will help you interact with the speakers. OSI gives you a platform to seek knowledge and associate with a lot of FOSS lovers. You will also get to meet and interact with the leaders in the open source domain. Open source is gradually taking over the tech world so make sure you stay updated with the evolving technology, interesting workshops and some really inspiring success stories.

We look forward to your presence! END

By: Manvi Saxena

The author is a part of the editorial group at EFY.

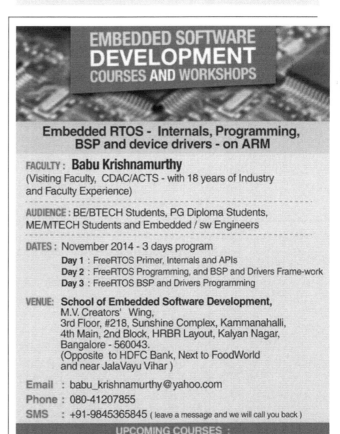

CODE SPORT

Sandya Mannarswamy

In this month's column, we feature a set of interview questions on algorithms, data structures, operating systems and computer architecture.

For the past few months, we have been discussing information retrieval, natural language processing (NLP) and the algorithms associated with them. In this month's column, we take a break from our discussion on NLP and explore a bunch of computer science interview questions.

1. You are asked to write a small code snippet in C to determine whether your computer is a little endian machine or a big endian machine. Assume that you can compile and run your C code using your favourite compiler on this computer. Is it possible for you to determine the endianness by looking at the assembly code without running the program? If not, explain how you can determine the endianness of the machine by running your code snippet.

2. You are running a C program and from the console you see that your program terminated with a 'stack overflow' signal error. When would a stack overflow signal be generated?

3. We all know that physical memory is volatile and, hence, when there is a power failure or system shutdown, contents of the physical memory are lost. Is it possible to have non-volatile physical memory? What are the different types of non-volatile physical memory?

4. If your computer has non-volatile physical memory instead of volatile physical memory, can you explain what would be the major operating system support needed to enable an application to restart from where it crashed?

5. Why do computer systems have multiple levels of cache hierarchy instead of a single large huge cache? Is it possible for an application to bypass the cache and read/write directly from the main memory?

6. We are all very familiar with Moore's law, which can be approximately stated as: "The transistor count on a processor chip doubles every 18 months." This has been resulting in the approximate doubling of processor speeds till now. However, over the last five years, there has been considerable talk about the end of Moore's law. What are the factors that are causing the end of Moore's law? Can you explain what the term 'dark silicon' means?

7. What is meant by 'Non-Uniform Memory Access (NUMA)' systems? If you have written a C application that runs on your personal computer, do you need to make changes to it in order for it to run on a NUMA system? If yes, what changes are needed? If not, explain why no changes are needed.

8. Given the wide prevalence of Android mobile devices today, what is the operating system running on these devices? If you have written a Java program that runs on your personal computer, can you run it without any changes on your Android mobile system? If not, explain why it can't be run, as is.

9. We all know that the data present on our laptops and personal computers is typically organised into files and directories. What are the different storage abstractions that are available on Android mobile devices for mobile applications to store data?

10. Many computer systems today have both a CPU and GPU built in to the same system, in what is known as 'Heterogeneous System Architecture (HSA)'. Is it possible for the same memory address space to be shared by the CPU and GPU? If yes, explain how it can be shared. If not, explain how data will be transferred between CPU and GPU.

11. We are familiar with various search algorithms such as Breadth First Search (BFS) and Depth First Search (DFS). If you are asked to pick a specific search algorithm to be run on a machine that is limited by the amount of physical memory available, which search algorithm

would you prefer and why?

12. What is meant by a 'topological sort' of a directed acyclic graph? Can you write an algorithm for it? If you run the topological sort algorithm on a directed graph which may contain cycles, what can you expect?

13. We are all familiar with algorithms for finding the shortest path in a graph such as Dijkstra's algorithm, which belongs to a category known as greedy algorithms. Can you explain what is meant by a greedy algorithm? Is it possible to come up with one for all programming problems?

14. What is the difference between the algorithmic complexity of classes P and NP? Given any problem, is it always possible to come up with an algorithm of complexity class P to solve it? If not, can you provide an example of a problem that is not known to have a solution of complexity class P?

15. Given a sentence in the English language consisting of words, how will you reverse the order of words in that sentence? For example, given the input sentence "Source control code system used by Linux kernel is Git," the program should output the sentence "Git is kernel Linux by used system code control source."

16. You are given a sorted array A of integers. You are asked to find out whether there are two indices 'i' and 'j' such that A[i] + A[j] = 0. What is the complexity of your solution?

17. What is the order of complexity of the following operations on a singly linked list: (a) Insertion (b) Deletion (c) Delete-minimum, and (d) Search for a specific value?

18. Is it always possible to transform a recursive function into a function containing an iterative loop? If not, give an example of when this transformation is not possible.

19. If you are given a single threaded application, and are asked to reduce its execution time, what would your approach be for the same?

20. Consider the following problem: you are given the task of identifying all the primes that exist between 1 and 8000000. You are also given a routine known as IsPrime, which when given an integer, returns true if it is a prime; else, it returns false. Given that you have access to a 64-core multi-processor system, how would you parallelise your application?

21. In problem (19), you were asked to find all primes that exist between 1 and 8000000. Now, if you are asked to find all primes that exist between 1 and 100, would your solution change?

22. What is the 'time of check to time of use' (TOCTOU) race condition? Given the potential for TOCTOU race conditions in file systems, what are the ways of preventing them?

23. Given the wide variety of synchronisation mechanisms available on Linux such as mutex, spinlock, semaphore, reader-writer lock and RCU, how would you decide which synchronisation mechanism to use for protecting a critical section of code in your application?

24. Given a binary search tree T containing N integers, and a value 'k', can you write an algorithm to find the predecessor and successor of 'k' in the tree T? Can there be a situation where the tree 'T' does not contain the predecessor to 'k'? Can there be a situation where the tree 'T' does not contain the successor to 'k'?

25. Consider a multi-threaded program executing on a multi-core system with N threads. Now, one of the threads in the program receives a SIGSEGV (segmentation violation) due to referencing an illegal memory address. What would happen to the application?

26. What is the worst case time complexity of the following operations on stack: (a) Insertion (b) Deletion (c) Delete-minimum, and (d) Search for a specific value?

27. What is the worst case complexity of a sorting algorithm? Is it possible to have a sorting algorithm which can sort in linear time? If yes, what are the additional assumptions that need to be enforced to ensure sorting in linear time?

28. You are asked to compute the factorial of a number N, where N is very large. You have the choice of either: (a) using recursion to compute the factorial, or (b) of remembering the solutions of earlier iterations in a memorisation table and computing the result by using the formula factorial (N) = factorial(N-1) * N by looking up the table for the value of factorial (N-1). Which of these two choices would be efficient in terms of: (a) the time complexity of the solution, or (b) the space complexity of the solution?

29. Given an array of N integers, how many comparisons are needed for finding the maximum? If you are asked to find both the minimum and maximum, how many comparisons are needed?

30. We are all familiar with the problem of a deadlock in concurrent code and we know how it can be detected and prevented. Assume that you have a concurrent application in which there is no circular wait among the threads. We know that if there is no circular wait, then the application cannot suffer from deadlock. Is it possible for the application to suffer from 'livelock'? If yes, explain how?

If you have any favourite programming questions/ software topics that you would like to discuss on this forum, please send them to me, along with your solutions and *feedback, at sandyasm_AT_yahoo_DOT_com.* Till we meet again next month, happy Diwali and happy programming! END

By: Sandya Mannarswamy

The author is an expert in systems software and is currently working with Hewlett Packard India Ltd. Her interests include compilers, multi-core and storage systems. If you are preparing for systems software interviews, you may find it useful to visit Sandya's LinkedIn group 'Computer Science Interview Training India' at http://www.linkedin.com/groups?home=HYPERLINK "http://www.linkedin.com/groups?home=&gid=2339182"&HYPERLINK "http://www.linkedin.com/groups?home=&gid2339182"gid=2339182

Anil Seth

Exploring Big Data on a Desktop: Elasticsearch on OpenStack

This column explores the use of the powerful, open source, distributed search tool, Elasticsearch, which can enable the retrieval of data through a simple search interface.

When you have a huge number of documents, wouldn't it be great if you could search them almost as well as you can with Google? Lucene (*http://lucene.apache.org/*) has been helping organisations search their data for years. Projects like Elasticsearch (*http://www.elasticsearch.org/*) are built on top of Lucene to provide distributed, scalable solutions in order to search huge volumes of data. A good example is the use of Elasticsearch at WordPress (*http://gibrown.wordpress.com/2014/01/09/scaling-elasticsearch-part-1-overview/*).

In this experiment, you start with three nodes on OpenStack: *h-mstr*, *h-slv1* and *h-slv2* as in the previous article. Download the rpm package from the Elasticsearch site and install it on each of the nodes.

The configuration file is */etc/elasticsearch/elasticsearch.yml*. You will need to configure it on each of the three nodes. Consider the following settings on the *h-mstr* node:

```
cluster.name: es
node.master: true
node.data: true
index.number_of_shards: 10
index.number_of_replicas: 0
```

We have given the name *es* to the cluster. The same value should be used on the *h-slv1* and *h-slv2* nodes. The *h-mstr* node will act as a master and store data as well. The master nodes process the requests by distributing the search to the data nodes and consolidating the results. The next two parameters relate to the index. The number of shards is the number of sub-indices that are created and distributed among the data nodes. The default value for the number of shards is 5. The number of replicas represents the additional copies of the indices created. Since it has been set to *No replicas*, the default value is 1.

You may use the same values on *slv1* and *slv2* nodes or use *node.master* set to *False*. Once you have loaded the data, you will find that the *h-mstr* node has four shards and *h-slv1* and *h-slv2* have three shards each. The indices will be in the directory */var/lib/elasticsearch/es/nodes/0/indices/* on each node.

You start Elasticsearch on each node by executing the following command:

```
$ sudo systemctl start elasticsearch
```

You can get to know the status of the cluster by browsing *http://h-mstr:9200/_cluster/health?pretty*.

Loading the data

If you want to index the documents located on your desktop, Elasticsearch supports a Python interface for it. It is available in the Fedora 20 repository. So, on your desktop, install:

```
$ sudo yum install python-elasticsearch
```

The following is a sample program to index LibreOffice documents. The comments embedded in the code hopefully make it clear that this is not a complex task.

```
#!/usr/bin/python
import sys
import os
import subprocess
from elasticsearch import Elasticsearch

FILETYPES=['odt','doc','sxw','abw']
# Covert a document file into a text file in /tmp and return
the text file name
def convert_to_text(inpath,infile):
    subprocess.call(['soffice','--headless','--convert-
to','txt:Text',
            '--outdir','/tmp','/'.join([inpath,infile])])
    return '/tmp/' + infile.rsplit('.',1)[0] + '.txt'
# Read the text tile and return it as a string
def process_file(p,f):
    textfile = convert_to_text(p,f)
    return ' '.join([line.strip() for line in open(textfile)])
# Search all files in a root path and select the document files
def get_documents(path):
    for curr_path,dirs,files in os.walk(path):
        for f in files:
            try:
                if f.rsplit('.',1)[1].lower() in FILETYPES:
                    yield curr_path,f
            except:
                pass
# Run this program with the root directory.
```

```
# If none, then the current directory is used.
def main(argv):
    try:
        path=argv[1]
    except IndexError:
        path='.'
    es = Elasticsearch(hosts='h-mstr')
    id = 0
# index each document with 3 attributes:
# path, title (the file name) and text (the text content)
    for p,f in get_documents(path):
        text = process_file(p,f)
        doc = {'path':p, 'title':f, 'text':text}
        id += 1
        es.index(index='documents', doc_type='text',id=id,
body= doc)
if __name__=="__main__":
    main(sys.argv)
```

Once the index is created, you cannot increase the number of shards. However, you can change the replication value as follows:

```
$ curl -XPUT 'h-mstr:9200/documents/_settings' -d '
{
    "index" : {
        "number_of_replicas" : 1
    } }
'
```

Now, the number of shards will be 7, 7 and 6, respectively, on the three nodes. As you would expect, if one of the nodes is down, you will still be able to search the documents. If more than one node is down, the search will return a partial result from the shards that are still available.

Searching the data

The program *search_documents.py* below uses the *query_string* option of Elasticsearch to search for the string passed as a parameter in the content field 'text'. It returns the fields 'path' and 'title' in the response, which are combined to print the full file names of the documents found.

```
#!/usr/bin/python
import sys
from elasticsearch import Elasticsearch
def main(query_string):
    es = Elasticsearch(['h-mstr'])
    query_body = {'query':
            {'query_string':
             { 'default_field':'text',
               'query': query_string}},
             'fields':['path','title']
             }
    # response is a dictionary with nested dictionaries
    response = es.search(index='documents', body=query_body)
    for hit in response['hits']['hits']:
        print '/'.join(hit['fields']['path'] + hit['fields']
['title'])
# run the program with search expression as a parameter
if __name__=='__main__':
    main(' '.join(sys.argv[1:]))
```

You can now search using expressions like the following:

```
$ python search_documents.py smalltalk objects
$ python search_documents.py smalltalk  AND objects
$ python search_documents.py +smalltalk  objects
$ python search_documents.py +smalltalk  +objects
```

More details can be found at the Lucene and Elasticsearch sites.

Open source options let you build a custom, scalable search engine. You may include information from your databases, documents, emails, etc, very conveniently. Hence, it is a shame to come across sites that do not offer an easy way to search their content. One hopes that website managers will add that functionality using tools like Elasticsearch! **END**

By: Anil Seth

The author has earned the right to do what interests him. You can find him online at *http://sethanil.com, http://sethanil. blogspot.com,* and reach him via email at *anil@sethanil.com*

The Basics of **Binary Exploitation**

Binary exploitation works on the principle of turning a weakness into an advantage. In this article, the author deals with the basics of binary exploitation.

Binary exploitation involves taking advantage of a bug or vulnerability in order to cause unintended or unanticipated behaviour in the problem.

Basics required for binary exploitation

Binary exploitation might appear to be a strange topic but once you get started on it, you won't be able to stop. To get started, you need to know how the process memory is organised and how the stack is framed.

Processes are mainly divided into three regions: the text region, data region, and stack region.

The text region contains the data of the program and the executable file. You can only read the data and if you to try to write the data, it will throw up a segment violation.

For easy understanding, the data segment is divided into three segments: data, BSS and heap. The data region contains global and static variables used in the program. The segment is further classified into two areas—for read-only data and the read-write area. The BSS segment has (uninitialised data) all global variables and static variables that are initialised to zero. Heap is usually managed by *malloc, free, realloc*, etc, where dynamic memory allocation is done

Stack is a type of abstract data type and it is LIFO (Last In First Out). It has a continuous block of memory containing data. The entire operations of the stack are controlled by the kernel. It is a continuous block of memory containing data in which the bottom of the

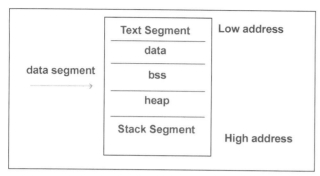

Figure 1: The overall process

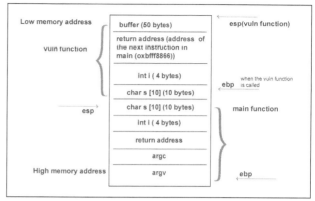

Figure 2: The stack

memory is fixed (higher memory address). Mainly, there are two operations in the collection of data, which are 'push' and 'pop'. The addition of an entity to the stack is a 'push' and the subtraction of an entity is a 'pop'. The register pointing to the top of the stack is the stack pointer (SP), which changes automatically based on the operation, and the register pointing to the bottom of the stack is the base pointer (BP). With the help of a small code snippet, we can see how the stack is framed.

```
#include<stdio.h>
int add(int , int);
int main(int argc , char **argv)
{
    int i;
    int j;
    int sum;
    sum= add(i,j);
    printf("Sum of two numbers = %d",sum); //assume that the
address is 0xbfff8866
    return 0;
}
int add(int i , int j)
{
    int sum;
    sum=i+j;
    return sum;
}
Figure 2 depicts how the stack is framed for the above
problem.
```

The GNU debugger

Most of you might be familiar with the *printf* debugger, which can only be used if you have the source code. But for the GNU debugger, you just need the executable file to see what is happening 'inside' the program.

Here is a list of commands that are frequently used in *gdb*.

```
1>prompt > gdb.
```

This is to get started with *gdb*.

```
2> (gdb) file executable filename
```

This gives the executable file name, which you need to debug.

```
3> (gdb) run
```

...is to run the program in *gdb*.

```
4> (gdb) kill
```

...is used to kill the program being debugged.

```
5> (gdb)disass function name\
```

...disassembles the function into the assembler.

```
6> (gdb)b (line number) or (function name) or *(address)
```

...sets break points at certain points of the code.

It is very important to learn how to do this last bit because while doing exploitations, you need to set break points and analyse how the program behaves.

```
7> (gdb) x/o(octal) or x(hex) or d(decimal) or u(unsigned
decimal) or t(binary) or f(float) or a(address) or
i(instruction) or c(char) and s(string) (string name) or
$(register name)
```

This is used to examine the memory of the code. Let's take a look at an example. *x/1s* s gives you what is in string 's'.

```
8> (gdb)info files or breakpoints or registers.
```

...will print the list of break points, files or registers.

```
9> (gdb)help command
```

With the command name and help argument, *gdb* displays a short paragraph on how to use that command.

A buffer overflow

A buffer overflow happens when a program tries to store more data than the actual size of the buffer. In such a case, the data overflows from the buffer, which leads to overwriting of the adjacent memory fragments of the process, as well as overwriting of the values of the IP (Instruction Pointer) or BP (Base Pointer) or other registers. This causes exceptions and segmentation faults, leading to other errors.

The problem given in the code snippet below will give you an idea about buffer overflows.

```
#include<stdio.h>
int main()
{
    char buffer[50];
    buffer[60]='a';
    return 0;
}
```

When you compile the above problem, the compiler will not throw you an error because there is no automatic bound checking on the buffer. But when you try to see the output of the program, it throws up a segmentation fault.

In buffer overflow attacks, the hacker tries to take advantage of extra memory segments for other operation instruction sets to inject malicious arbitrary code such as shell codes, and the pre-determined program behaviour is changed eventually. To exploit buffer overflows, you need to have some idea of assembly code instructions and you should get control over the eip register. Getting control over eip is very simple—you just need to know how the stack is framed and know where the eip register is located. Getting control of *gdb* also helps you to find the eip register. Once you get control over eip you can return to any point in the code and get arbitrary things like the shell.

A buffer overflow also occurs due to some vulnerabilities in the problem. Normally, buffer overflow vulnerabilities are found through source code analysis, or by reverse engineering application binaries.

With the help of this small problem, let us look at how a buffer overflow could possibly occur.

```
#include<stdio.h>
#include<string.h>
void function(char *string)
{
char buffer[50];
strcpy(buffer,string);
}
int main(int argc, char **argv)
{
```

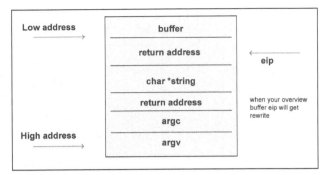

Figure 3: Buffer overflow

```
    function(argv[1]);
    return 0;
}
```

Figure 3 clearly describes the above problem.

In the above problem, if the input is less than 50 characters, then the program will execute normally. When 50 characters are exceeded, the compiler throws up a segmentation fault. The above problem describes how the vulnerability *strcpy* leads to an overflow.

To get started up with buffer overflows, it would be good if you start up with *picoctf*. Once you are familiar with it, you can 'smash the stack'.

Shell code

In most of the binary exploitation problems, we just have to capture the shell, so we need to know a little bit about how to write shell code. As of now, we can modify the return address (which is just the address of eip) by just overflowing the buffer. In most cases, you just need to spawn the shell. From the shell, you can execute the command as you like. With the help of this small code snippet in C, you will get the shell.

```
#include<stdio.h>
int main()
{
    system("/bin/sh");
}
```

When you compile the above code in a terminal, you will get a shell. Writing the code in C language is simple, but when you need to inject it in a buffer, it should be in ASCII as you cannot inject the code in C into the buffer. It is not that necessary to learn to write shell code in ASCII because of online availability. The online resource for shell code is *http://shell-storm.org/shellcode/* END

By: Rakesh Paruchuri

The author is a security enthusiast.

Deploying Infrastructure-as-a-Service Using OpenStack

Cloud computing is the buzzword today. It has many different models, one of which is IaaS. In this article, the authors describes the delivery of IaaS using open source software OpenStack.

Nowadays, cloud computing has become mainstream both in the research as well as corporate communities. A number of cloud services providers offer computing resources in different domains as well as forms. Cloud computing refers to the delivery of computing resources as a service rather than as a product. In cloud services, the computing power, devices, resources, software and information are delivered to clients as utilities. Classically, such services are provided and transmitted by using network infrastructure or simply delivered over the Internet.

Infrastructure as-a-service (IaaS)

IaaS includes the delivery of computing infrastructure such as a virtual machine, disk image library, raw block storage, object storage, firewalls, load balancers, IP addresses, virtual local area networks and other features on-demand from a large pool of resources installed in data centres. Cloud providers bill for the IaaS services on a utility computing basis; the cost is based on the amount of resources allocated and consumed.

OpenStack: a free and open source cloud computing platform

OpenStack is a free and open source, cloud computing software platform that is widely used in the deployment of infrastructure-as-a-Service (IaaS) solutions. The core technology with OpenStack comprises a set of interrelated projects that control the overall layers of processing,

storage and networking resources through a data centre that is managed by the users using a Web-based dashboard, command-line tools, or by using the RESTful API.

Currently, OpenStack is maintained by the OpenStack Foundation, which is a non-profit corporate organisation established in September 2012 to promote OpenStack software as well as its community. Many corporate giants have joined the project, including GoDaddy, Hewlett Packard, IBM, Intel, Mellanox, Mirantis, NEC, NetApp, Nexenta, Oracle, Red Hat, SUSE Linux, VMware, Arista Networks, AT&T, AMD, Avaya, Canonical, Cisco, Dell, EMC, Ericsson, Yahoo!, etc.

OpenStack users

• AT&T	• Purdue University
• Stockholm University	• Red Hat
• SUSE	• CERN
• Deutsche Telekom	• HP Converged Cloud
• HP Public Cloud	• Intel
• KT (formerly Korea Telecom)	• NASA
• NSA	• PayPal
• Disney	• Sony
• Rackspace Cloud	• SUSE Cloud Solution
• Wikimedia Labs	• Yahoo!
• Walmart	• Opera Software

OpenStack releases with the components included
OpenStack Austin - Nova, Swift
OpenStack Bexar - Nova, Glance, Swift
OpenStack Cactus - Nova, Glance, Swift
OpenStack Diablo - Nova, Glance, Swift
OpenStack Essex - Nova, Glance, Swift, Horizon, Keystone
OpenStack Folsom - Nova, Glance, Swift, Horizon, Keystone, Quantum, Cinder
OpenStack Grizzly - Nova, Glance, Swift, Horizon, Keystone, Quantum, Cinder
OpenStack Havana - Nova, Glance, Swift, Horizon, Keystone, Neutron, Cinder, Heat, Ceilometer
OpenStack Icehouse - Nova, Glance, Swift, Horizon, Keystone, Neutron, Cinder, Heat, Ceilometer, Trove

OpenStack computing components

OpenStack has a modular architecture that controls large pools of compute, storage and networking resources.

Compute (Nova): OpenStack Compute (Nova) is the fabric controller, a major component of Infrastructure as a Service (IaaS), and has been developed to manage and automate pools of computer resources. It works in association with a range of virtualisation technologies. It is written in Python and uses many external libraries such as Eventlet, Kombu and SQLAlchemy.

Object storage (Swift): It is a scalable redundant storage system, using which objects and files are placed on multiple disks throughout servers in the data centre, with the OpenStack software responsible for ensuring data replication and integrity across the cluster. OpenStack Swift replicates the content from other active nodes to new locations in the cluster in case of server or disk failure.

Block storage (Cinder): OpenStack block storage (Cinder) is used to incorporate continual block-level storage devices for usage with OpenStack compute instances. The block storage system of OpenStack is used to manage the creation, mounting and unmounting of the block devices to servers. Block storage is integrated for performance-aware scenarios including database storage, expandable file systems or providing a server with access to raw block level storage. Snapshot management in OpenStack provides the authoritative functions and modules for the back-up of data on block storage volumes. The snapshots can be restored and used again to create a new block storage volume.

Networking (Neutron): Formerly known as Quantum, Neutron is a specialised component of OpenStack for managing networks as well as network IP addresses. OpenStack networking makes sure that the network does not face bottlenecks or any complexity issues in cloud deployment. It provides the users continuous self-service capabilities in the network's infrastructure. The floating IP addresses allow traffic to be dynamically routed again to any resources in the IT infrastructure, and therefore the users can redirect traffic during maintenance or in case of

Figure 1: OpenStack

any failure. Cloud users can create their own networks and control traffic along with the connection of servers and devices to one or more networks. With this component, OpenStack delivers the extension framework that can be implemented for managing additional network services including intrusion detection systems (IDS), load balancing, firewalls, virtual private networks (VPN) and many others.

Dashboard (Horizon): The OpenStack dashboard (Horizon) provides the GUI (Graphical User Interface) for the access, provision and automation of cloud-based resources. It embeds various third party products and services including advance monitoring, billing and various management tools.

Identity services (Keystone): Keystone provides a central directory of the users, which is mapped to the OpenStack services they are allowed to access. It refers and acts as the centralised authentication system across the cloud operating system and can be integrated with directory services like LDAP. Keystone supports various authentication types including classical username and password credentials, token-based systems and other log-in management systems.

Image services (Glance): OpenStack Image Service (Glance) integrates the registration, discovery and delivery services for disk and server images. These stored images can be used as templates. It can also be used to store and catalogue an unlimited number of backups. Glance can store disk and server images in different types and varieties of back-ends, including Object Storage.

Telemetry (Ceilometer): OpenStack telemetry services (Ceilometer) include a single point of contact for the billing systems. These provide all the counters needed to integrate customer billing across all current and future OpenStack components.

Orchestration (Heat): Heat organises a number of cloud applications using templates with the help of the OpenStack-native REST API and a CloudFormation-compatible Query API.

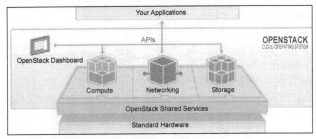

Figure 2: OpenStack: an open source cloud operating system
[Source: openstack.org]

Database (Trove): Trove is used as database-as-a-service (DaaS), which integrates and provisions relational and non-relational database engines.

Elastic Map Reduce (Sahara): Sahara is the specialised service that enables data processing on OpenStack-managed resources, including the processing with Apache Hadoop.

Deployment of OpenStack using DevStack

DevStack is used to quickly create an OpenStack development environment. It is also used to demonstrate the starting and running of OpenStack services, and provide examples of using them from the command line. DevStack has evolved to support a large number of configuration options and alternative platforms and support services. It can be considered as the set of scripts which install all the essential OpenStack services in the computer without any additional software or configuration. To implement DevStack, first download all the essential packages, pull in the OpenStack code from various OpenStack projects, and set everything for the deployment.

To install OpenStack using DevStack, any Linux-based distribution with 2GB RAM can be used to start the implementation of IaaS.

Here are the steps that need to be followed for the installation.

1. Install Git

```
$ sudo apt-get install git
```

2. Clone the DevStack repository and change the directory. The code will set up the cloud infrastructure.

```
$ git clone http://github.com/openstack-dev/devstack
$ cd devstack/
```

```
/devstack$ ls
```

```
accrc          exercises      HACKING.rst  rejoin-stack.sh  tests
AUTHORS        exercise.sh    lib          run_tests.sh     tools
clean.sh       extras.d       LICENSE      samples          unstack.sh
driver_certs   files          localrc      stackrc
eucarc         functions      openrc       stack-screenrc
exerciserc     functions-common  README.md    stack.sh
```

stack.sh, unstack.sh and *rejoin-stack.sh* are the most important files. *stack.sh* script is used to set up DevStack. *unstack.sh* is used to destroy the DevStack setup.

If you are on the earlier execution of *./stack.sh*, the environment can be brought up by executing the *rejoin_stack.sh* script.

3. Execute the *stack.sh* script:

```
/devstack$ ./stack.sh
```

Here, the MySQL database password is entered. There's no need to worry about the installation of MySQL separately

on this system. We have to specify a password and this script will install MySQL, and use this password there.

Finally, we will have the script ending as follows:

```
+ merge_config_group /home/r/devstack/local.conf post-extra
+ local localfile=/home/r/devstack/local.conf
+ shift
+ local matchgroups=post-extra
+ [[ -r /home/r/devstack/local.conf ]]
+ return 0
+ [[ -x /home/r/devstack/local.sh ]]
+ service_check
+ local service
+ local failures
+ SCREEN_NAME=stack
+ SERVICE_DIR=/opt/stack/status
+ [[ ! -d /opt/stack/status/stack ]]
++ ls '/opt/stack/status/stack/*.failure'
++ /bin/true
+ failures=
+ '[' -n '' ']'
+ set +o xtrace
```

- Horizon is now available at *http://1.1.1.1/*
- Keystone is serving at *http://1.1.1.1:5000/v2.0/*
- Examples on using the *novaclient* command line are in *exercise.sh*
- The default users are: admin and demo
- The password: nova
- This is your host IP: *1.1.1.1*

After all these steps, the machine becomes the cloud service providing platform. Here, *1.1.1.1* is the IP of my first network interface.

We can type the host IP provided by the script into a browser, in order to access the dashboard 'Horizon'. We can log in with the username 'admin' or 'demo' and the password 'admin'.

You can view all the process logs inside the screen, by typing the following command:

```
$ screen -x
```

Executing the following will kill all the services, but it should be noted that it will not delete any of the code.

To bring down all the services manually, type:

```
$ sudo killall screen
```

localrc configurations

localrc is the file in which all the local configurations (local machine parameters) are maintained. After the first successful *stack.sh* run, you will see that a *localrc* file gets created with the configuration values you specified while running that script.

The following fields are specified in the *localrc* file:

DATABASE_PASSWORD
RABBIT_PASSWORD
SERVICE_TOKEN
SERVICE_PASSWORD
ADMIN_PASSWORD

If we specify the option *OFFLINE=True* in the *localrc* file inside DevStack directory, and if after specifying this, we run *stack.sh*, it will not check any parameter over the Internet. It will set up DevStack using all the packages and code residing in the local system. In the phase of code development, there is need to commit the local changes in the */opt/stack/nova* repository before restack (re-running *stack.sh*) with the *RECLONE=yes* option. Otherwise, the changes will not be committed.

To use more than one interface, there is a need to specify which one to use for the external IP using this configuration:

```
HOST_IP=xxx.xxx.xxx.xxx
```

Cinder on DevStack

Cinder is a block storage service for OpenStack that is designed to allow the use of a reference implementation (LVM) to present storage resources to end users that can be consumed by the OpenStack Compute Project (Nova). Cinder is used to virtualise the pools of block storage devices. It delivers end users with a self-service API to request and use the resources, without requiring any specific complex knowledge of the location and configuration of the storage where it is actually deployed.

All the Cinder operations can be performed via any of the following:

1. CLI (Cinder's *python-cinderclient* command line module)
2. GUI (Using OpenStack's GUI project *horizon*)
3. Direct calling of Cinder APIs

Creation and deletion of volumes: To create a 1 GB Cinder volume with no name, run the following command:

```
$ cinder create 1
```

To see more information about the command, just type *cinder help <command>*

```
$ cinder help create

usage: cinder create [--snapshot-id <snapshot-id>]
                     [--source-volid <source-volid>]
[--image-id <image-id>]
                     [--display-name <display-name>]
                     [--display-description <display-
description>]
                     [--volume-type <volume-type>]
                     [--availability-zone <availability-
zone>]
                     [--metadata [<key=value> [<key=value>
```

```
...]]]
                         <size>
Add a new volume.
Positional arguments:
  <size>                Size of volume in GB
Optional arguments:
  --snapshot-id <snapshot-id>
                        Create volume from snapshot id
(Optional,
                        Default=None)
  --source-volid <source-volid>
                        Create volume from volume id
(Optional, Default=None)
  --image-id <image-id>
                        Create volume from image id
(Optional, Default=None)
  --display-name <display-name>
                        Volume name (Optional, Default=None)
  --display-description <display-description>
                        Volume description (Optional,
Default=None)
  --volume-type <volume-type>
                        Volume type (Optional, Default=None)
  --availability-zone <availability-zone>
                        Availability zone for volume
(Optional, Default=None)
  --metadata [<key=value> [<key=value> ...]]
                        Metadata key=value pairs (Optional,
Default=None)
```

To create a Cinder volume of size 1GB with a name, using *cinder create --display-name myvolume:*

```
$ cinder create --display-name myvolume 1
```

Property	Value
attachments	[]
availability_zone	nova
bootable	false
created_at	time
display_description	None
display_name	myvolume
id	id
metadata	{}
size	1
snapshot_id	None
source_volid	None
status	creating
volume_type	None

To list all the Cinder volumes, using *cinder list:*

```
$ cinder list
```

ID	Status	Display Name	Size	Volume type	Bootable	Attached To
id1	Available	Myvolume	1	None	False	
id2	Available	None	1	None	False	

To delete the first volume (the one without a name), use the *cinder delete <volume_id>* command. If we execute *cinder list* really quickly, the status of the volume going to 'deleting' can be seen, and after some time, the volume will be deleted:

```
$ cinder delete id2
```

```
$ cinder list
```

ID	Status	Display Name	Size	Volume type	Bootable	Attached To
id1	Available	Myvolume	1	None	False	
id2	Deleting	None	1	None	False	

Volume snapshots can be created as follows:

```
$ cinder snapshot-create id2
+---------------------+-----------------------------+
|       Property      |            Value            |
+---------------------+-----------------------------+
|     created_at      |          TimeStamp          |
| display_description |            None             |
|    display_name     |            None             |
|         id          |          snapshot2          |
|      metadata       |             {}              |
|        size         |             1               |
|       status        |          creating           |
|     volume_id       |            id2              |
+---------------------+-----------------------------+
```

All the snapshots can be listed as follows:

```
$ cinder snapshot-list
```

ID	Volume ID	Status	Display Name	Size
Snapshotid1	id2	Available	None	1

You can also create a new volume of 1GB from the snapshot, as follows:

```
$ cinder create --snapshot-id snapshotid1 1
+---------------------+-----------------------------+
|       Property      |            Value            |
+---------------------+-----------------------------+
|     attachments     |             []              |
|  availability_zone  |            nova             |
|      bootable       |           false             |
|     created_at      |        creationtime         |
| display_description |            None             |
|    display_name     |            None             |
|         id          |             v1              |
|      metadata       |             {}              |
|        size         |             1               |
|     snapshot_id     |         snapshotid1         |
|    source_volid     |            None             |
|       status        |          creating           |
|    volume_type      |            None             |
+---------------------+-----------------------------+
```

There are lots of functions and features available with OpenStack related to cloud deployment. Depending upon the type of implementation, including load balancing, energy optimisation, security and others, the cloud computing framework OpenStack can be explored a lot **END**

By: Dr Gaurav Kumar and Amit Doegar

Dr Gaurav Kumar is the MD of Magma Research & Consultancy Pvt Ltd, Ambala. He is associated with a number of academic institutes in delivering expert lectures and conducting technical workshops on the latest technologies and tools. E-mail: *kumargaurav.in@gmail.com*

Amit Doegar is an assistant professor in the National Institute of Technical Teachers' Training and Research at Chandigarh. He can be contacted at *amit@nitttrchd.ac.in*

Writing I2C Clients in LINUX

I2C is a protocol for communication between devices. In this column, the author takes the reader through the process of writing I2C clients in Linux.

I2C is a multi-master synchronous serial communication protocol for devices. All devices have addresses through which they communicate with each other. The I2C protocol has three versions with different communication speeds – 100kHz, 400kHz and 3.4MHz. The I2C protocol has a bus arbitration procedure through which the master is decided on the bus, and then the master supplies the clock for the system and reads and writes data on the bus. The device that is communicating with the master is the slave device.

The Linux I2C subsystem

The Linux I2C subsystem is the interface through which the system running Linux can interact with devices connected on the system's I2C bus. It is designed in such a manner that the system running Linux is always the I2C master. It consists of the following subsections.

I2C adapter: There can be multiple I2C buses on the board, so each bus on the system is represented in Linux using the *struct i2c_adapter* (defined in *include/linux/i2c.h*). The following are the important fields present in this structure.

bus number: Each bus in the system is assigned a number that is present in the I2C adapter structure which represents it.

I2C algorithm: Each I2C bus operates with a certain protocol for communicating between devices. The algorithm that the bus uses is defined by this field. There are currently three algorithms for the I2C bus, which are pca, pcf and bitbanging. These algorithms are used to communicate with devices when the driver requests to write or read data from the device.

I2C client: Each device that is connected to the I2C bus on the system is represented using the *struct i2c_client* (defined in *include/linux/i2c.h*). The following are the important fields present in this structure.

Address: This field consists of the address of the device on the bus. This address is used by the driver to communicate with the device.

Name: This field is the name of the device which is used to match the driver with the device.

Interrupt number: This is the number of the interrupt line of the device.

I2C adapter: This is the *struct i2c_adapter* which represents the bus on which this device is connected. Whenever the driver makes requests to write or read from the bus, this field is used to identify the bus on which this transaction is to be done and also which algorithm should be used to communicate with the device.

I2C driver: For each device on the system, there should be a driver that controls it. For the I2C device, the corresponding driver is represented by *struct i2c_driver* (defined in *include/linux/i2c.h*). The following are the important fields defined in this structure.

Driver.name: This is the name of the driver that is used to match the I2C device on the system with the driver.

Probe: This is the function pointer to the driver's probe routine, which is called when the device and driver are both found on the system by the Linux device driver subsystem.

To understand how to write I2C device information and the I2C driver, let's consider an example of a system in which there are two devices connected on the I2C bus. A description of these devices is given below.

Device 1

Device type: EEPROM
Device name: eeprom_xyz
Device I2C address: 0x30
Device interrupt number: 4
Device bus number: 2

Device 2

Device type: Analogue to digital converter
Device name: adc_xyz
Device I2C address: 0x31
Device interrupt number: Not available
Device bus number: 2

Writing the I2C device file

I2C devices connected on the system are represented by *struct i2c_client*. This structure is not directly defined but, instead, *struct i2c_board_info* is defined in the board file. *struct i2c_client* is defined using struct *i2c_board_info* structure by the Linux I2C subsystem, the fields of the *i2c_board_info* object is copied to *i2c_client* object created.

> **Note:** Board files reside in *arch/ folder* in Linux. For example, the board file for the ATSTK1000 board of the AVR32 architecture is *arch/avr32/boards/atstk1000.c* and the board file for Beagle Board of ARM OMAP3 architecture is *arch/arm/mach-omap2/board-omap3beagle.c.*

struct i2c_board_info (defined in *include/linux/i2c.h*) has the following important fields.

type: This is the name of the I2C device for which this structure is defined. This will be copied to the name field of *i2c_client object* created by the I2C subsystem.

addr: This is the address of the I2C device. This field will be copied to address the field of *i2c_client object* created by the I2C subsystem.

irq: This is the interrupt number of the I2C device. This field will be copied to the *irq* field of the *i2c_client object* created by the I2C subsystem.

An array of *struct i2c_board_info* object is created, where each object represents the I2C device connected on the bus. For our example system, the *i2c_board_info* object is written as follows:

```
static struct i2c_board_info xyz_devices[] = {
    {
        .type = "eeprom_xyz",
        .addr = 0x30,
```

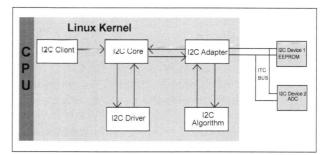

Figure 1: Linux I2C system

```
        .irq = 4,
    },
    {
        .type = "adc_xyz",
        .addr = 0x31,
    },
};
```

I2C device registration

I2C device registration is a process with which the kernel is informed about the device present on the I2C bus. The I2C device is registered using the *struct i2c_board_info* object defined. The kernel gets information about the device's address, bus number and name of the device being registered. Once the kernel gets this information, it stores this information in its global linked list *__i2c_board_list*, and when the *i2c_adapter* which represents this bus is registered, the kernel creates the *i2c_client* object from this *i2c_board_info* object.

I2C device registration is done in the board *init* code present in the board file. I2C devices are registered in the Linux kernel using the following two methods.

Case 1: In most cases, the bus number on which the device is connected is known; in this case the device is registered using the bus number. When the bus number is known, I2C devices are registered using the following API:

```
int i2c_register_board_info(int busnum, struct i2c_board_info
*info, unsigned len);
```

…where,

busnum = the number of the bus on which the device is connected. This will be used to identify the *i2c_adapter* object for the device.

info = array of *struct i2c_board_info* object, which consists of information of all the devices present in the bus.

len = number of elements in the info array.

For our example system, I2C devices are registered as follows:

```
i2c_register_board_info(2, xyz_devices, ARRAY_SIZE(xyz_
devices));
```

What the *i2c_register_board_info* does is link the *struct i2c_board_info* object in *__i2c_board_list*, which is the global linked list.

Now, when the I2C adapter is registered using *i2c_register_adapter* API (defined in drivers/i2c/i2c-core.c), it will search for devices that have the same bus number as the adapter, through the *i2c_scan_static_board_info* API. When the *i2c_board_info* object is found with the bus number which is the same as that of the adapter being registered, a new *i2c_client* object is created using the *i2c_new_device* API.

The *i2c_new_device* API creates a new *struct i2c_client* object and the fields of the *i2c_client* object are initialised with the fields of the *i2c_board_info* object. The new *i2c_client* object is then registered with the I2C subsystem. During registration, the kernel matches the name of all the I2C drivers with the name of the I2C client created. If any I2C driver's name matches with the I2C client, then the probe routine of the I2C driver will be called.

Case 2: In some cases, instead of the bus number, the *i2c_adapter* on which the device is connected is known; in this case, the device is registered using the *struct i2c_adapter* object.

When the *i2c_adapter* is known instead of the bus number, the I2C device is registered using the following API:

```
struct i2c_client *
 i2c_new_device(struct i2c_adapter *adap, struct i2c_board_
info const *info);
```

...where,

adap = i2c_adapter representing the bus on which the device is connected.

info = i2c_board_info object for each device.

In our example, the device is registered as follows.
For device 1:

```
i2c_new_device(adap, &xyz_devices[0]);
```

For device 2:

```
i2c_new_device(adap, &xyz_devices[1]);
```

Writing the I2C driver

As mentioned earlier, generally, the device files are present in the *arch/xyz_arch/boards* folder and similarly, the driver files reside in their respective driver folders. For example, typically, all the RTC drivers reside in the *drivers/rtc* folder and all the keyboard drivers reside in the *drivers/input/keyboard* folder.

Writing the I2C driver involves specifying the details of the *struct i2c_driver*. The following are the required fields for *struct i2c_driver* that need to be filled:

driver.name = name of the driver that will be used to match the driver with the device.

driver.owner = owner of the module. This is generally the *THIS_MODULE* macro.

probe = the probe routine for the driver, which will be called when any I2C device's name in the system matches with this driver's name.

Note: It's not just the names of the device and driver that are used to match the two. There are other methods to match them such as *id_table* but, for now, let's consider their names as the main parameter for matching. To understand the way in which the ID table is used, refer to the Linux source code.

For our example of the EEPROM driver, the driver file will reside in the *drivers/misc/eeprom* folder and we will give it a name—*eeprom_xyz.c*. The *struct i2c_driver* will be written as follows:

```
static struct i2c_driver eeprom_driver = {
        .driver = {
                    .name = "eeprom_xyz",
          .owner = THIS_MODULE,
        },
        .probe = eeprom_probe,
};
```

For our example of an *adc* driver, the driver file will reside in the *drivers/iio/adc* folder, which we will name as *adc_xyz.c*, and the *struct i2c_driver* will be written as follows:

```
static struct i2c_driver adc_driver = {
      .driver = {
        .name = "adc_xyz",
        .owner = THIS_MODULE,
      },
       .probe = adc_probe,
};
```

The *struct i2c_driver* now has to be registered with the I2C subsystem. This is done in the *module_init* routine using the following API:

```
i2c_add_driver(struct i2c_driver *drv);
```

...where *drv* is the *i2c_driver* structure written for the device.

For our example of an EEPROM system, the driver will be registered as:

```
i2c_add_driver(&eeprom_driver);
```

...and the *adc* driver will be registered as:

```
i2c_add_driver(&adc_driver);
```

What this *i2c_add_driver* does is register the passed driver with the I2C subsystem and match the name of the driver with all the *i2c_client names*. If any of the names match, then the probe routine of the driver will be called and the *struct i2c_client* will be passed as the parameter to the probe routine. During the probe routine, it is verified that the device represented by the *i2c_client* passed to the driver is the actual device that the driver supports. This is done by trying to communicate with the device represented by *i2c_client* using the address present in the *i2c_client* structure. If this fails, it returns an error from the probe routine informing the Linux device driver subsystem that the device and driver are not compatible; or else it continues with creating device files, registering interrupts and registering with the application subsystem.

The probe skeleton for our example EEPROM system will be as follows:

```
static int eeprom_probe(struct i2c_client *client, const
struct i2c_device_id *id)
{
    check if device exists;
    if device error
    {
        return error;
    }
    else
    {
        do basic configuration of eeprom using
        client->addr;

        register with eeprom subsystem;

        register the interrupt using client->irq;
    }
    return 0;
}


static int adc_probe(struct i2c_client *client, const struct
i2c_device_id *id)
{
    check if device exists;
    if device error
    {
        return error;
    }
    else
    {
        do basic configuration of adc using
        client->addr;

        register with adc subsystem;
    }
    return 0;
}
```

After the probe routine is called and all the required

configuration is done, the device is active and the user space can read and write the device using system calls. For a very clear understanding of how to write *i2c_driver*, refer to the drivers present in the Linux source code—for example, the RTC driver on *i2c bus*, the *drivers/rtc/rtc-ds1307.c* file and other driver files.

For reading and writing data on the I2C bus, use the following API.

Reading bytes from the I2C bus:

```
i2c_smbus_read_byte_data(struct i2c_client *client, u8
command);
```

client: i2c_client object received from driver probe routine.
command: the command that is to be transferred on the bus.

Reading words from the I2C bus:

```
i2c_smbus_read_word_data(struct i2c_client *client, u8
command);
```

client: i2c_client object received from driver probe routine.
command: the command that is to be transferred on the bus.

Writing bytes on an I2C bus:

```
i2c_smbus_write_byte_data(struct i2c_client *client, u8
command, u8 data);
```

client: i2c_client object received from driver probe routine.
command: the command that is to be transferred on the bus.
data: the data that is to be written to the device.

Writing words on an I2C bus:

```
i2c_smbus_write_word_data(struct i2c_client *client, u8
command, u16 data);
```

client: i2c_client object received from driver probe routine.
command: the command that is to be transferred on the bus.
data: the data that is to be written to the device
When the read or write command is issued, the request is completed using the adapters algorithm, which has the routines to read and write on the bus. **END**

References

[1] *http://lxr.missinglinkelectronics.com/linux/Documentation/i2c/*
[2] Video on 'Writing and submitting your first Linux kernel patch', *https://www.youtube.com/watch?v=LLBrBBlmJt4*
[3] 'Writing and submitting your first Linux kernel patch' (text file and presentation), *https://github.com/gregkh/kernel-tutorial*

By: Raghavendra Chandra Ganiga

The author can be contacted at *ravi23ganiga@gmail.com*

Try Your Hand at Owncloud Development

Owncloud is a free and open source file hosting software system. This article will introduce readers to it and also guide them on setting up an Owncloud developer environment.

O wncloud operates in a simple way to set up a cloud storage system (e.g., Dropbox) on your own website. Apart from being a cloud storage system like Dropbox, it allows people to make and share their own application software which has the capability of running their own Owncloud, including text editors, task lists and more. All of this makes it possible to get a little more out of Owncloud than just file syncing. Owncloud is an advanced version of Dropbox. Some of the applications which are currently available are files, documents, a photo gallery, a PDF viewer, music, mail, contacts, calendar, etc.

Frank Karlitschek developed Owncloud in 2010. His aim was to provide a free software replacement to proprietary storage service providers. This cloud storage has been integrated with the GNOME desktop. Integration of Owncloud with the Kolab groupware and collaboration project has been started recently. Groupware is an application software designed to help people involved in a common task to achieve goals, and Kolab is such a free and open source suite.

Owncloud makes it possible to specify a storage quota for users—the maximum space a user is allowed to use for files located in an individual's home storage. The storage space available is good enough for all kinds of users. Administrators need to be aware, while setting a quota, that it is only applicable to actual files and not to application metadata. This means that when allocating a quota, they should make sure there is at least 10 per cent more space available for a given user. For a beginner, these things don't matter.

One of the great things about Owncloud is that it is cross-platform, and a number of applications support it. Much of this is achieved because it is open source and uses open standards or defines open application interfaces. Owncloud provides access to your data through a Web interface and provides a platform to easily view, synchronise and share across devices under one's control. Owncloud's open architecture is extensible via a simple but powerful application interface and plug-ins, and works with any storage.

Installation

Generally, Owncloud is considered an online storage source like the very common Google Drive. The benefit of Owncloud is that the server is on a location that you install it to and not on someone else's server.

This guide assumes that a LAMP stack is installed and

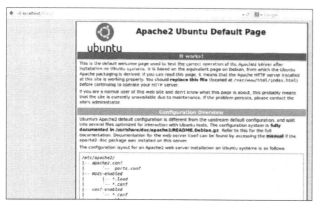

Figure 1: Local host

Figure 2: Owncloud on localhost

configured on the system. To check whether it is already installed, just try typing 'localhost' on your browser. If you see something like what's shown in Figure 1, then you are ready with the local host.

Now we can start with setting up the Owncloud developer environment.

Make a directory called *Owncloud* in a location where you have write permission, type the given code in your terminal, and execute it:

```
sudo mkdir /var/www/owncloud

sudo chown YOURUSERNAME:YOURGROUP /var/www/
owncloud
```

> **Note:** You should replace YOURUSERNAME:YOURGROUP with your own username and groupname.

```
chmod a+rw /var/www/owncloud
```

Now you should have a ready-to-develop set-up in your localhost. You can check it on *http://localhost/owncloud/ core/*. You will see something like what is shown in Figure 2.

Once you are ready with your set-up, you can clone the core. All source code is available on Github. So we can simply clone it from Github, for which you just follow the commands given below.

First, enter the *Owncloud* directory, which you have already created. For that, type the following command:

```
cd /var/www/owncloud
```

Now we have to clone into this directory from Git. To clone the core, type the following:

```
git clone https://github.com/owncloud/core.git
```

If you are planning to contribute or are interested in

working with Owncloud applications, then you can simply clone that also from Git. For that, type the following:

```
git clone https://github.com/owncloud/apps.git
```

You can now change your directory to core, and then type the following on your terminal to set up your developer environment:

```
cd core/
git submodule init
git submodule update
mkdir data
sudo chown -R www-data:www-data config/
sudo chown -R www-data:www-data data/
sudo chown -R www-data:www-data apps/
```

Once you are done with these steps, you will be able to access your Owncloud with its original credentials. You can store your files, etc, in the same setup.

Contributing to Owncloud

As I mentioned earlier, Owncloud started out in 2010. It's still under development and the community supports new contributors as well as beginners with essential requirements.

You can find Owncloud issues on Github. For beginners, I recommend that you start with minor jobs. Owncloud has been listed among GSoC (Google Summer of Code) participating organisations, and also on OPW (the FOSS Outreach Program for Women). The IRC channels of Owncloud are very active and are really helpful.

If you are interested in cloud computing or private clouds, I suggest you start contributing to Owncloud and feel the beauty of cloud computing. END

By: Anjana S

The author is an open source enthusiast. She can be reached at *anjanasasindran123@gmail.com*.

Understanding
jQuery Mobile's Page Structure

This article delves into jQuery Mobile, an HTML5-based framework for creating mobile Web applications, which works on all popular smartphones and tablets. The authors enhance the discussion by walking the reader through how to develop a Web app.

jQuery Mobile is a cross-platform, open source UI framework that enables developers to build websites and applications by integrating HTML5, CSS3 and layout foundation with very little scripting. The framework is compatible with every mobile device and tablet (more platform support can be found at *http://jquerymobile.com/gbs/*) including browsers such as Firefox, Chrome, Internet Explorer, Android, BlackBerry and Symbian.

What it is and what it is not

jQuery Mobile is built on top of jQuery, which means that it uses jQuery's core framework but doesn't replace it. Being lightweight makes it fast, robust and easily themeable - it allows us to build customised themes easily, and offers Ajax navigation with touch events, page transition, widgets and mouse navigation. jQuery Mobile is neither a SDK for packaging native Web apps, nor a framework for JavaScript, nor an alternative for Web browsers.

To get started, we need:
- A Web browser
- A text editor

How to use jQuery Mobile

There are basically two ways we can make use of jQuery Mobile:

1. Simply download the latest stable version of the download builder from *http://jquerymobile.com/download-builder/* , extract the folder to your working directory and provide the path for use in your code.
2. Using CDN (Content Delivery Network) distributes often-used files across the Web and, most importantly, it doesn't require any download.

It is assumed that the reader is familiar with HTML5 markup language and the basics of CSS.

jQuery Mobile's page structure

Create *index.html* and include jQuery Mobile library files in the header.

A page developed on jQuery Mobile must follow a series of rules for proper functioning. Every bit of content visible must be inside a container with the data-role attribute defined as *"page" usually div.*

First, declare the HTML5 doctype, viewpoint and width of the page inside the header. Viewpoint will ensure that your app appears correctly on all devices. Next, add the jQuery framework or library files either by downloading to the local folder or by loading files from CDN as shown in Figure 1.

Create a page using a data attribute

Define a 'page' using the HTML5 data-role attribute with

three important sections, namely, the header, content and footer, as shown below:

```
<div data-role="page">
<div data-role="header"> </div>
<div data-role="content"> </div>
<div data-role="footer" > </div>
</div>
```

Notice that in the above code snippet we used something called 'data-role'. It specifies which div/block should be used for the page, header, content and footer. Data-role assigns roles to regular HTML elements.

Now let's add some content to our 'page', 'header', 'content' and 'footer' to make a mobile Web app. First, add some theme to our 'page' using the data-theme:

```
<div data-role="page" data-theme="b"> or <div data-
role="page" class="ui-bar ui-bar-e">
```

jQuery Mobile supports some powerful themes. jQuery provides its own themes or, if needed, you can create your own theme. More information about themes can be found at *http://themeroller.jquerymobile.com/* .

Making our list of items searchable

Listview can be an ordered or unordered list on a page with at least one item in it. jQuery Mobile renders lists for touch devices and it automatically occupies the whole width of the page. Listview may also contain item separators, multiple lists and, most importantly, it must be made searchable.

Inside the *<ul>* tag, add *data-role "listview"* with *data-insert= "true"* to specify whether the element should be within content margins or outside of them. Once Listview is added, look at the search box above the list. This can be used to search any of the listed items. Try searching some country's name in the search bar after adding Listview.

```
<ul data-role="listview" data-insert="true" data-
filter="true">
```

Format the footer

Now that our header, content and search bar is looking good, let's add a footer to our page using *data-role= "footer"*, *data-position= "fixed"* (this attribute is used to keep the footer position fixed) inside the *<div>* tag.

```
<div data-role="footer" data-position="fixed" data-theme="e">
```

Last of all, add *data-role= "navbar"*. jQuery mobile provides a number of icons that can be used with the *"data-icon"* attribute or class named *"ui-icon-"*. jQuery provides both PNG and SVG images of icons. For example, the following will display the home icon at the footer (for more

Figure 1: jQuery Mobile library files capture

Figure 2: Final app

information on icons, refer to *http://api.jquerymobile.com/icons/*) and upon clicking the *Home* button, it will navigate to the first page using *href= "#MainPage"*.

```
<nav data-role="navbar">
    <ul>
        <li><a href="#MainPage" data-icon="home">Home</a></
li>
        <li><a href="settings" data-icon="gear">Settings</
a></li>
    </ul></nav>
```

Building a simple Web app

Now that we have some basic understanding of jQuery Mobile's page structure, let's create a simple app (Figure 2).

The complete code for our app follows. (Add the *<script>* code given below after defining jQuery Mobile library files.)

```
<head><script> <!-- JQuery script for our HTML5 code -->
    $(document).ready(function(){
    var loc = window.location.href;
    $("li").click(function(){
    var country = $(this).attr("id");
    $("#FlagImage").attr ("src", function (i,origValue){
    return "images\\" + country + "-flag.jpg";});
    $("#FlagDescription").text ("This is "+ country.
toUpperCase () +" Flag");
    $("#FlagHeader").text (country.toUpperCase () + " " +
"Flag");
    newURL = loc +"#FlagPage";
    $(location).attr('href',newURL); });}); </script></head>
<body>
    <div data-role="page" data-theme="a" id="MainPage">
        <header data-role="header" data-theme="b">
            <h1>National Flag</h1>
        </header><!-- /header -->
        <div data-role="content" data-theme="d">
```

```
            <ul data-role="listview" data-insert="true" data-
filter="true">
                <li id="india"><a> <h1>Indian National Flag</
h1></a></li>
                <li id="usa"><a> <h1>USA National Flag</h1></
a></li>
                <li id="england"><a> <h1>England National
Flag</h1></a></li>
                <li id="japan"><a> <h1>Japan National Flag</
h1></a></li>
                <li id="china"><a> <h1>China National Flag</
h1></a></li>
            </ul>
        </div><!-- /content -->
        <div data-role="footer" data-position="fixed" data-
theme="b">
            <nav data-role="navbar">
                <ul>
                    <li><a href="#MainPage" data-
icon="home">Home</a></li>
                    <li><a href="Info" data-
icon="info">Info</a></li>
                    <li><a href="plus" data-
icon="plus">Share</a></li>
                </ul>
            </nav>
        </div><!-- /footer -->
    </div><!-- /page -->
    <div data-role="page" id="FlagPage" data-theme="b">
        <div data-role="header">
            <h1 id="FlagHeader"> Header </h1>
            <a href="#MainPage" data-icon="arrow-l">Back</a>
```

```
        </div>
        <div class="img">
            <img id="FlagImage"/>
            <p id="FlagDescription"></p>
        </div>
        <div data-role="footer" data-position="fixed" data-
theme="b">
            <nav data-role="navbar">
                <ul>
                    <li><a href="#MainPage" data-
icon="home">Home</a></li>
                    <li><a href="Info" data-
icon="info">Info</a></li>
                    <li><a href="plus" data-
icon="plus">Share</a></li>
                    <li><a href="settings" data-
icon="gear">Settings</a></li>
                </ul>
            </nav>
        </div><!-- /footer -->
    </div>
</body>
</html> END
```

By: Vinay Patkar and Avinash Bendigeri

Vinay works as a software development engineer at Dell India R&D Centre, Bengaluru, and has close to two years' experience in automation, Windows Server OS. He is interested in virtualisation and cloud computing technologies.

Avinash, too, works as a software development engineer at Dell R&D Centre, Bengaluru. He is interested in the automation and systems management domains.

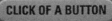

Exploring a Few Type Classes in Haskell

Haskell, an open source programming language, is the outcome of 20 years of research. It is named after the logician, Haskell Curry. It has all the advantages of functional programming and an intuitive syntax based on mathematical notation. Let's continue our exploration of Haskell.

In this article, we shall explore more type classes in Haskell. Consider the *Functor* type class:

```
class Functor f where
    fmap :: (a -> b) -> f a -> f b
```

It defines a function *fmap*, which accepts a function as an argument that takes input of *Type a* and returns *Type b*, and applies the function on every *Type a* to produce *Type b*. The *f* is a type constructor. An array is an instance of the *Functor* class and is defined as shown below:

```
instance Functor [] where
    fmap = map
```

The *Functor* type class is used for types that can be mapped over. Examples of using the *Functor* type class for arrays are shown below:

```
ghci> fmap length ["abc", "defg"]
[3,4]

ghci> :t length
```

```
length :: [a] -> Int

ghci> map length ["abc", "defg"]
[3,4]

ghci> :t map
map :: (a -> b) -> [a] -> [b]
```

An instance of a *Functor* class must satisfy two laws. First, it must satisfy the identity property where running the map over an ID must return the id. The term 'id' represents identity.

```
fmap id = id
```

For example:

```
ghci> id ["abc"]
["abc"]

ghci> fmap id ["abc"]
["abc"]
```

Second, if we compose two functions and *fmap* over it,

then it must be the same as mapping the first function with the *Functor*, and then applying the second function as shown below:

```
fmap (f . g) = fmap f . fmap g
```

This can also be written for a *Functor F* as follows:

```
fmap (f . g) F = fmap f (fmap g F)
```

For example:

```
ghci> fmap (negate . abs) [1, 2, 3, 4, 5]
[-1,-2,-3,-4,-5]
```

```
ghci> fmap negate (fmap abs [1, 2, 3, 4, 5])
[-1,-2,-3,-4,-5]
```

The *Maybe* data type can also be an instance of the *Functor* class:

```
data Maybe a = Just a | Nothing
     deriving (Eq, Ord)
```

```
instance Functor Maybe where
    fmap f (Just x) = Just (f x)
    fmap f Nothing = Nothing
```

For example:

```
ghci> fmap (+2) (Nothing)
Nothing
```

```
ghci> fmap (+2) (Just 3)
Just 5
```

The two laws hold good for the *Maybe* data type:

```
ghci> id Nothing
Nothing
```

```
ghci> id Just 4
Just 4
```

```
ghci> fmap (negate . abs) (Just 4)
Just (-4)
```

```
ghci> fmap negate (fmap abs (Just 4))
Just (-4)
```

The *Applicative* type class is defined to handle cases where a function is enclosed in a Functor, like Just (*2):

```
class Functor f => Applicative f where
    -- | Lift a value.
```

```
    pure :: a -> f a

    -- | Sequential application.
    (<*>) :: f (a -> b) -> f a -> f b
```

The '<$>' is defined as a synonym for 'fmap':

```
(<$>) :: Functor f => (a -> b) -> f a -> f b
f <$> a = fmap f a
```

The *Applicative Functor* must also satisfy a few mathematical laws. The *Maybe* data type can be an instance of the *Applicative* class:

```
instance Applicative Maybe where
    pure = Just
    (Just f) <*> (Just x) = Just (f x)
    _        <*> _        = Nothing
```

A few examples of *Maybe* for the *Applicative* type class are shown below:

```
ghci> import Control.Applicative

ghci> Just (+2) <*> Just 7
Just 9

ghci> (*) <$> Just 3 <*> Just 4
Just 12

ghci> min <$> Just 4 <*> Just 6
Just 4

ghci> max <$> Just "Hello" <*> Nothing
Nothing

ghci> max <$> Just "Hello" <*> Just "World"
Just "World"
```

The *Applicative Functor* unwraps the values before performing an operation.

For a data type to be an instance of the *Monoid* type class, it must satisfy two properties:
1. Identity value
2. Associative binary operator
a * (b * c) = (a * b) * c

These are defined in the *Monoid* type class:

```
class Monoid a where
    mempty :: a             -- identity
    mappend :: a -> a -> a -- associative binary operation
```

Lists can be a *Monoid*. The identity operator is [] and the associative binary operator is (++). The instance definition of lists for a *Monoid* is given below:

```
instance Monoid [a] where
    mempty = []
    mappend = (++)
```

Some examples of lists as *Monoid* are shown below:

```
ghci> import Data.Monoid

ghci> ("a" `mappend` "b") `mappend` "c"
"abc"

ghci> "a" `mappend` ("b" `mappend` "c")
"abc"

ghci> mempty `mappend` [5]
[5]
```

The *Monad* type class takes a wrapped value and a function that does some computation after unwrapping the value, and returns a wrapped result. The *Monad* is a container type and hence a value is wrapped in it. The *bind* operation (>>=) is the important function in the *Monad* class that performs this operation. The 'return' function converts the result into a wrapped value. *Monads* are used for impure code where there can be side effects, for example, during a system call, performing IO, etc. A data type that implements the *Monad* class must obey the Monad Laws. The definition of the *Monad* class is as follows:

```
class Monad m where
  (>>=) :: m a -> (a -> m b) -> m b
  (>>) :: m a -> m b -> m b
  return :: a -> m a
  fail :: String -> m a
```

The *Maybe* type is an instance of a *Monad* and is defined as:

```
instance Monad Maybe where
    return x = Just x
    Nothing >>= f = Nothing
    Just x >>= f = f x
    fail _ = Nothing
```

So, when 'm' is *Maybe*, and 'a' and 'b' are of *Type Int*, the bind operation becomes:

```
(>>=) :: Maybe Int -> (Int -> Maybe Int) -> Maybe Int
```

Here's an example of how the *Maybe Monad* is used:

```
ghci> return (Just 5)
Just 5
```

```
ghci> return Nothing
Nothing

ghci> Just 5 >>= \x -> return (x + 7)
Just 12

ghci> Nothing >>= \x -> return (x + 7)
Nothing

ghci> Just 5 >>= \x -> return (x + 7) >>= \y -> return (y + 2)
Just 14
```

The *newtype* keyword is used in Haskell to define a new data type that has only one constructor and only one field inside it. The *Writer* data type can be defined using the record syntax as follows:

```
newtype Writer w a = Writer { runWriter :: (a, w) }
```

It can be an instance of a *Monad* as follows:

```
import Data.Monoid

newtype Writer w a = Writer { runWriter :: (a, w) }

instance (Monoid w) => Monad (Writer w) where
    return x = Writer (x, mempty)
    (Writer (x,v)) >>= f = let (Writer (y, v')) = f x in Writer (y, v `mappend` v')
```

To test the definition, you can write a double function as shown below:

```
double :: Int -> Writer String Int
double x = Writer (x * 2, " doubled " ++ (show x))
```

You can execute it using:

```
ghci> runWriter $ double 3
(6," doubled 3")

ghci> runWriter $ double 3 >>= double
(12," doubled 3 doubled 6")
```

The evaluation for the bind operation is illustrated below:

```
ghci> runWriter $ double 3 >>= double
(12," doubled 3 doubled 6")

ghci> runWriter $ ((double 3) >>= double)
(12," doubled 3 doubled 6")

ghci> runWriter $ ((Writer (6, "doubled 3")) >>= double)
(12," doubled 3 doubled 6")
```

The arguments to *runWriter* are matched to the *bind* function definition in the *Writer Monad*. Thus, x == 6, v == 'doubled 3', and f == 'double'. The function application of 'f x' is 'double 6' which yields '(12, "doubled 6")'. Thus y is 12 and v' is 'doubled 6'. The result is wrapped into a *Writer Monad* with y as 12, and the string v concatenated with v' to give 'doubled 3 doubled 6'. This example is useful as a logger, where you want a result and log messages appended together. As you can see, the output differs with input, and hence this is impure code that has side effects.

When you have data types, classes and instance definitions, you can organise them into a module that others can reuse. To enclose the definitions inside a module, prepend them with the module keyword. The module name must begin with a capital letter followed by a list of types and functions that are exported by the module. For example:

```
module Control.Monad.Writer.Class (
    MonadWriter(..),
    listens,
    censor,
) where

...
```

You can import a module in your code or at the GHCi prompt, using the following command:

```
import Control.Monad.Writer
```

If you want to use only selected functions, you can selectively import them using:

```
import Control.Monad.Writer(listens)
```

If you want to import everything except a particular function, you can hide it while importing, as follows:

```
import Control.Monad.Writer hiding (censor)
```

If two modules have the same function names, you can explicitly use the fully qualified name, as shown below:

```
import qualified Control.Monad.Writer
```

You can then explicitly use the 'listens' functions in the module using *Control.Monad.Writer.listens*. You can also create an alias using the 'as' keyword:

```
import qualified Control.Monad.Writer as W
```

You can then invoke the 'listens' function using *W.listens*.

Let us look at an example of the iso8601-time 0.1.2 Haskell package. The module definition is given below:

```
module Data.Time.ISO8601
  ( formatISO8601
  , formatISO8601Millis
  , formatISO8601Micros
  , formatISO8601Nanos
  , formatISO8601Picos
  , formatISO8601Javascript
  , parseISO8601
  ) where
```

It then imports a few other modules:

```
import Data.Time.Clock (UTCTime)
import Data.Time.Format (formatTime, parseTime)
import System.Locale (defaultTimeLocale)
import Control.Applicative ((<|>))
```

This is followed by the definition of functions. Some of them are shown below:

```
-- | Formats a time in ISO 8601, with up to 12 second decimals.
--
-- This is the `formatTime` format @%FT%T%Q@ == @%%Y-%m-%dT%%H:%M:%S%Q@.
formatISO8601 :: UTCTime -> String
formatISO8601 t = formatTime defaultTimeLocale "%FT%T%QZ" t

-- | Pads an ISO 8601 date with trailing zeros, but lacking the trailing Z.
--
-- This is needed because `formatTime` with "%Q" does not create trailing zeros.
formatPadded :: UTCTime -> String
formatPadded t
  | length str == 19 = str ++ ".000000000000"
  | otherwise        = str ++ "000000000000"
  where
    str = formatTime defaultTimeLocale "%FT%T%Q" t

-- | Formats a time in ISO 8601 with up to millisecond precision and trailing zeros.
-- The format is precisely:
-- >YYYY-MM-DDTHH:mm:ss.sssZ
formatISO8601Millis :: UTCTime -> String
formatISO8601Millis t = take 23 (formatPadded t) ++ "Z"

...
```

The availability of free and open source software allows you to learn a lot from reading the source code, and it is a very essential practice if you want to improve your programming skills. END

By: Shakthi Kannan

The author is a free software enthusiast and blogs at *shakthimaan.com*.

Automate the Provisioning Process for Cloud Inventory

This article describes how to automate the provisioning of cloud inventory on *www. digitalocean.com* and is based on how the author's own company went about doing so.

The SaaS offering from Sastra Technologies, a firm that I co-founded, promises customers their very own database, which means that each customer has a separate database for its operational data. This puts a lot of pressure on our engineering team to ensure the database is provisioned and the SaaS widgets are up and running within minutes of the customers signing up. In the beginning, we were inclined to run a few shell scripts and have these set up by an engineer; however, we soon realised that our customers are based in the UK and could sign up while we were asleep. We had to enable this by automating the entire provisioning process. We initially looked at Puppet, Chef and FAI but these solutions had a pricing plan and, being a start-up, our aim was to conserve funds. So we decided to roll out our own provisioning scripts using the Digital Ocean API.

The case for automation

We had several compelling reasons for automating our provisioning. The primary reason was to guard ourselves against our inability to scale and provide infrastructure in case there was a flood of sign ups, especially in the middle of the night. Automation would also ensure that subsequent environments would be identical to those set up previously —this is important because we didn't want components to fail due to differences in the versions of the underlying infrastructure components.

The background

Digital Ocean (DO) is a cloud computing provider and is ranked 15th among hosting companies in terms of Web-facing computers, according to a news item in Netcraft (*http://news.netcraft.com/archives/2013/12/11/digitalocean-*

now-growing-faster-than-amazon.html) and as of writing this article, has just announced a new region in London.

As a company, we host on several of its servers. The rest of this article is about our experience in automatically provisioning the DO infrastructure.

An overview of the Digital Ocean API (DO API)

The Digital Ocean API is a RESTful API, which means that users can access the functions using HTTP methods. The API allows you to manage the resources in a programmatic way—you can create new droplets (instances), resize them, install additional packages and do a lot more.

The solution diagram

Figure 1 gives a view of the various components that were included in the technology stack. Those highlighted are the ones that need to horizontally scale out and the rest of this article discusses how we accomplished this.

Rolling out the shell script using the DO API

To roll out your own scripts you will need to know UNIX shell programming, some Python and the Digital Ocean API reference. We chose to use Python because of its simple but powerful command set. You will also need to register and set up a Digital Ocean account. Though not an absolute necessity, prior experience in setting up the infrastructure would help. So let's get started by creating our first Droplet programmatically.

Spinning a new Droplet

The first step in provisioning is to instantiate a virtual server, which Digital Ocean calls a Droplet; so let's first spin a Droplet. Fire up your editor, key in the following Python code and save it as *DON-Droplet.py*

```
def main(DropletName):
    SizeID = GetSizeID ('2GB')
    OSID  = Geomagnetic ("CentOS 6.4 x32")
    RegID = GetRegID ('Singapore 1')
    SshID = GetSSH('sridhar@sridhar-Aspire-5745')
    if (SizeID == "ERROR" or OSID == "ERROR" or RegID ==
"ERROR" or SshID  == "ERROR"):
        print "Size/OS/Region/Ssh ID Not Found. So Exiting..."
        return
    print "Size ID::[" + SizeID + "] OS ID::[" + OSID + "]
Region ID::[" + RegID + "] SSH ID::[" + SshID + "]"
    print "Creation of Droplet::[...Start"
    print "DropLet Name::[" + DropletName + "]"
    CreateDroplet (DropletName, SizeID, OSID, RegID, SshID)
    print "Creation of Droplet...End"
    return
```

The main function allows us to specify the size of the Droplet (yes, for now we have hardcoded it!), the image ID

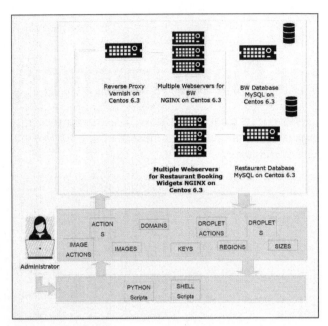

Figure 1: Solution diagram

of the OS that you want to install, the ID of the region in which you want to create your Droplet and the SSH keys that you want to install. Each of these values is passed to the respective functions to check if they are valid before we create the Droplet with those values. For example, to check if the size we have specified is valid and available, we use the following function:

```
def GetSizeID (SizeName):
    RespArr = GetDON ('sizes')
    if RespArr == "ERROR":
      print "Problem in getting sizes from DON."
      return "ERROR"
    for RespRow in RespArr:
      RespRow = Clean (RespRow)
      #print "arr entries->", RespRow
      Flds = dict (Fld.split (":") for Fld in RespRow.split
(","))
      if Flds['name'] == SizeName:
        print "Size::[" + SizeName + "] id::[" +
Flds['id'] + "]. Found"
        return Flds['id'].strip()
    print "Size::[" + SizeName + "] Not Found."
    return "ERROR"
```

We query the API with GetDON ('sizes') to get the list of the available sizes. The API returns an array with the list of available sizes and we parse the array to check if we have the size that's specified by the user in the main function. If we have the required size, the rest of the checks like Image ID and Region ID are performed by the respective functions: GetImageID ("CentOS 6.4 x32"), GetRegID ('Singapore 1'), and GetSSH (sridhar@sridhar-Aspire-5745). If any of these checks fail, we abort Droplet creation. If the checks are successful, we proceed to create the Droplet using *CreateDroplet (DropletName, SizeID, OSID, RegID, SshID)*.

The Python function to create a Droplet takes the name, size, OS Image ID, Region ID and the SSH key as arguments, and uses the RESTful API to create the Droplet. A word of caution: the API keys provided here are dummy keys, just for illustrating the flow of the code. You will have to obtain your keys by registering with Digital Ocean.

```
def CreateDroplet (Name, Size, OS, Reg, Passkey):
    #Copying DON's Parameters..
    data = {}

    data['client_id'] = 'xj53GXMazSf3NCCznoL'
    data['api_key'] = '941c3d1a0240e900ae450848c94'

    data['name'] = Name
    data['size_id'] = Size
    data['image_id'] = OS
    data['region_id'] = Reg
    data['ssh_key_ids'] = Passkey
    URL_Values = urllib.urlencode(data)

    #Connect to DON for values of APIKey...
    URL = 'https://api.digitalocean.com/droplets/new?'
    Full_URL = URL + URL_Values
    print "Droplet Creation URL->[" + Full_URL + "]."
    print "Connecting DON to create droplet"
    print "URL Execution Start..."
    data = urllib2.urlopen(Full_URL)
    DON_Result = data.read()
    print "Droplet Creation Response::[" + DON_Result + "]"
    print "URL Execution End."
    return
```

That's all it takes to create a Droplet. Since we used an SSH key, the root password will not be emailed to us. Log in to the new Droplet using SSH and you'll be prompted for the password since we haven't yet disabled the password authentication in *sshd_conf* configuration. So you'll have to go to the Web console and request for your password or you should not use the SSH keys while creating the Droplet!

Let's now create the users we require and install our infrastructure components—MySQL, PHP, NGINX, Munin, APC, Memcached and Postfix.

Setting up a Droplet

Before installing the components, first set up the time zone, create users, add them to a group and set up the firewall rules. In our case, we set up the time zone to IST, created users, added them to WHEEL (so that they have super cow powers), and then closed all ports except those we required. You can create this as a shell script called *droplet-admin.bash* or download it from *www.opensourcefoyu.com/articles/article_source_code/nov14/cloud_inventory.zip*. Run the script to make the above changes or you can do it one by one.

Deploying the cloud stack

Let us now write a script to install PHP Fast CGI, MySQL, Nginx, APC, memcached and Munin.

Let's start with the script for installing the PHP-fCGI. Choose fCGI instead of the conventional PHP module as the former is known to have a lower memory footprint. Create a *php-install.bash* file with the following contents:

```
yum install php php-fpm -y
rpm -ivh http://dl.fedoraproject.org/pub/epel/6/x86_64/epel-
release-6-8.noarch.rpm
yum install php-mcrypt -y
yum install php-gd php-imap -y
echo 'cgi.fix_pathinfo=0' >> /etc/php.ini
echo 'date.timezone = America' >> /etc/php.ini
service php-fpm start
service php-fpm status
```

This script installs *php php-fpm*. It then downloads the *php-mcrypt*, *php-gd*, *php-impa* from the *epel* repositories and installs them. *Php-fpm* requires the *cgi.fix_pathinfo=0* to be set in the *php.ini* file, which is done by the *echo* command. The script then automatically starts *php-fpm*.

After PHP, the next thing to be installed is MySQL. Create *mysql-install.bash* by using the following commands:

```
yum install mysql mysql-server -y
chkconfig --levels 235 mysqld on
service mysqld start
service mysqld status
```

The script installs MySQL and configures it to start up automatically when the server starts up. The script currently doesn't remove the demo database. You might want to include that step.

NGINX is not available from the official Centos repositories and the official package has to be downloaded from the NGINX site. Create *nginx-install.bash* with the following lines. This will enable the appropriate repositories and install NGINX:

```
wget http://nginx.org/packages/rhel/6/noarch/RPMS/nginx-
release-rhel-6-0.el6.ngx.noarch.rpm
rpm -ivh nginx-release-rhel-6-0.el6.ngx.noarch.rpm
yum install nginx -y
chkconfig nginx on
service nginx start
service nginx status
```

Our next step is to install APC or the Alternate PHP Cache, which is available in PECL. Create *apc-install.bash* with the following lines. This will install APC.

```
yum install php-pear php-devel httpd-devel pcre-devel gcc
make -y
pecl install apc
echo "extension=apc.so" > /etc/php.d/apc.ini
```

Next, we need to install *memcached*. Just create *memcached-install.bash* with the following command:

```
yum install memcached -y
```

Any technology stack requires to be monitored, for which we use *munin*. To install *munin*, create *munin-install.bash* with the following commands:

```
yum --enablerepo=epel install munin munin-node -y
/etc/init.d/munin-node start
chkconfig munin-node on
service munin-node status
```

We now have the individual scripts to install the various components of our stack. We can create a master script *infra-install.py* to chain these individual shell scripts. You can download *infra-install.py* from *www.opensourcefoyu.com/articles/article_source_code/nov14/cloud_inventory.zip*

To provision your Droplet and have it ready, all you need to do is to run *infra-install.py* (ensure all your scripts have the requisite permissions for executing it).

Other methods

The other method of provisioning hosting infrastructure is to use one of the several products available like Puppet *(https://puppetlabs.com/)*, Chef *(http://www.getchef.com/)*, CFEngine *(https://cfengine.com/)*, Cobbler *(http://www.cobblerd.org/)*, FAI *(http://fai-project.org/)*, Kickstart *(http://www.centos.org)*, BCFG2 *(http://bcfg2.org/)* or Vagrant *(http://www.vagrantup.com/)*

Scope for improvement

For the sake of brevity, we have included the essential commands to get you started on auto-scaling your infrastructure. But there are a few things that you should include to improve these scripts.

Currently, we have to log in once before we execute the other commands because though we have provided SSH keys for the root user at the time of creating the Droplet, we haven't disabled password authentication in the *sshd_config* file.

Though we create users, the script doesn't automatically copy the public keys for the users. You can add a few commands to automatically copy the SSH keys to the respective HOME directories and disable the password authentication mechanism.

After installing MySQL, it is a good practice to remove the test databases and anonymous users. The script currently doesn't do this.

You can add AWStats to the list of infrastructure components.

You might want to run this suite of scripts as a Jenkins Job instead of manually running it. **END**

References

[1] *https://developers.digitalocean.com/* provides a detailed guide for developers to navigate the API calls.

By: Jaysingh T and Sridhar Pandurangiah

Jaysingh T is a Technical Manager with SCOPE International Standard Chartered Bank. He can be contacted at: *jayasinght@ymail.com*

Sridhar Pandurangiah is the co-founder and director of Sastra Technologies, a start-up engaged in providing EDI solutions on the cloud. He can be contacted at: *sridhar@sastratechnologies.in /sridharpandu@gmail.com.* He maintains a technical blog at *sridharpandu.wordpress.com*

All About a **Configuration Management Tool Called Chef**

Explore Chef, the open source tool that streamlines the task of configuring and maintaining a company's servers. Written in Ruby and Erlang, it can easily integrate with cloud-based platforms to automatically provision and configure new machines.

Chef is an open source tool and framework that provides developers and systems administrators a foundation of APIs and libraries, which are used to perform tasks such as configuring and managing IT infrastructures. The concept behind using framework technology is to reduce development time by minimising the overhead of implementing and managing the low-level details that support the development effort. This enables organisations to concentrate on delivery and meeting the customers' requirements.

Chef is a framework for infrastructure development, which provides a supporting structure and package for framing one's infrastructure as code. It provides extensive libraries for building up an infrastructure that can be deployed within a software project. It provides a Ruby-based DSL modelling infrastructure, which enables developers and systems administrators to build and design scalable environments without considering the operating systems. It produces consistent, shareable and reusable components.

Chef provides various tools built on the framework for designing the infrastructure. These tools are based on high level programming languages such as Python and Ruby. Some of the tools are:

1) *Ohai*, a system profiling tool, which is an extendable plug-in to furnish the data that is used to build up the database of each system that is managed by Chef.
2) *Shef*, an interactive debugging console for testing and exploring Chef's behaviour in various conditions. It provides command line access to framework libraries.
3) *Chef-Solo*, a configuration management tool, which allows access to subsets of Chef's features.
4) *Chef Client*, an agent that runs on the system managed by Chef to communicate with the Chef server.
5) *Knife*, a multi-purpose command line tool, which provides system automation, integration, and deployment.

A few features of Chef

- It manages a huge amount of nodes on a single Chef server.
- It maintains a blueprint of the entire infrastructure.
- It can be easily managed using operating systems such as Linux, Windows, FreeBSD and Solaris.
- It integrates with all major cloud service providers.
- High availability.
- Centralised management, i.e., a single Chef server can be used as the centre for deploying the policies.
- It provides a Web-based management console to control the access of objects such as nodes, cookbooks and so on.

How Chef works

Chef converts infrastructure into code. Whatever operations can be done with the code, can be done with the infrastructure as well. Yes, it is possible to keep infrastructure versions, test them and create infrastructure repeatedly and efficiently.

A resource is a definition of an action that can be taken such as the installation of a package, Web server or application server; or managing a configuration file. Chef uses reusable components known as recipes to automate infrastructure. A recipe is a collection of resources that includes packages, templates and so on. A cookbook is a set of recipes such as the installation of the Web server, the database server, and configuration file changes to connect the Web and database servers in different deployment environments. A workstation is the place where the Knife is configured to upload cookbooks to the Chef server. Chef's command-line tool, Knife, is used to interact with the Chef server and upload cookbooks. Attributes provide specific details of a node, such as the IP address and other configuration details.

The Chef server is the central registry or brain of the entire process and can act as a hub. It consists of information about the infrastructure and cookbooks. The latter are used to instruct Chef on how each node must be configured. The Chef server can be either hosted on-premise, on the cloud or be offered by

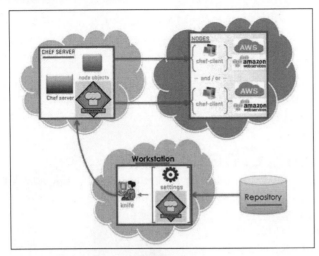

Figure 1: How Chef works with AWS nodes

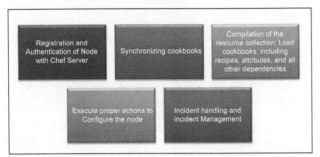

Figure 2: The Chef client

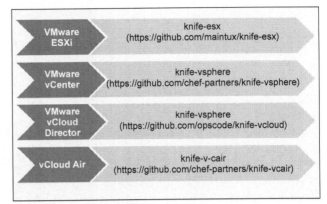

Figure 3: Chef plug-in for VMware

some service provider as well. It is used to deploy cookbooks to the nodes. There is an option of signing up for Opscode's Hosted Chef. Each node is registered with the Chef server, which distributes cookbooks to the nodes based on different configuration settings.

The Chef client is installed on the nodes; it contacts the Chef server, fetches cookbooks and executes them on nodes. The Chef client does the actual configuration. It polls the Chef server at regular intervals for the most recent recipes, and checks node compliance with the policy defined by the most recent recipes. If the node is out of sync, the Chef client runs the policy on the node to bring it up-to-date. A node can be a physical server, a virtual server or a virtual machine in a private cloud or public cloud environment. Many plug-ins are available for Knife that provide support for cloud-based environments. Amazon EC2, Amazon Virtual Private Cloud, VMware, Google Compute Engine, OpenStack, Rackspace and Microsoft Azure are supported cloud platforms or cloud-based environments. A Chef client is an agent that runs locally on every node hosted in different environments, and follows the steps shown in Figure 2.

Chef, VMware, AWS and continuous delivery

A Chef and VMware-based private cloud

Chef is the configuration management tool and an automation platform for installing, configuring and managing VMware infrastructure. It can be used to automate the entire stack including provisioning and de-provisioning VMs, templates and networks.

vCloud Air is a public cloud platform built on the foundation of vSphere. It is compatible with the on-premises data centre. It allows organisations to extend workloads into the cloud or to migrate existing onsite virtual machines to the public cloud. Chef can be used to automate migrations to vCloud Air. Chef has the capability of provisioning new vCloud Air VMs and bootstrap, as well as list the vCloud Air VMs, vApps, templates or images, networks, NAT rules, firewall rules and public IP addresses.

VMware vCenter Server is a centralised management tool to manage virtualisation environments based on VMware vSphere. It can be used to manage multiple ESXi servers and virtual machines with a single console application. It provides enterprise level features such as high availability and fault tolerance with VMotion, Storage VMotion and Distributed Resource Scheduler. The *knife-esx* plug-in gives you full control of ESX-hosted virtual machines. Chef's *knife-vsphere* plug-in is used to provision and manage VMs with VMware vCenter. The *knife-vsphere* plug-in can be used to list data stores, resource pools and clusters; to list, clone, and delete VMs; perform specific actions by executing commands on deployed virtual machines; to customise or reconfigure vCPUs, VRAM, and IP addresses to clone a VM; and to clone and bootstrap Linux VMs and Windows VMs.

VMware ESXi is an enterprise-level operating system-independent hypervisor offered by VMware. It is a Type 1 hypervisor for guest virtual machines. It runs on a physical host without an underlying operating system support and hence it gives better performance than Type 2 hypervisors. Chef can be used to provision/de-provision or manage virtual machines hosted by ESXi. The *knife-esx* plug-in is used to integrate Chef with ESXi.

Advantages of Chef in a VMware environment

There are many advantages of using Chef in a VMware environment as listed below:

- Write once, deploy many times
- No manual configurations
- No inconsistencies in environment
- Standardised run time environment; application deployment, middleware and databases

Chef and the Amazon public cloud

Chef and Amazon public cloud integration makes infrastructure fast and agile. The *knife-ec2* plug-in is used to integrate AWS and Chef. It allows cloud consumers to launch and configure EC2 instances, to create base Amazon Machine Images, to register EC2 instances with Elastic Load Balancers, to manage EBS volumes and raid devices. It is very easy to spin off a Windows 2012 server, configure IIS and deploy a .NET app in AWS with the use of Chef, which provides speed and efficiency with standard environments. In AWS, it is very easy to maximise the uptime of the Chef server by taking advantage of Chef's integration with Amazon's elastic block storage and elastic IPs. Different AWS regions can also be used to gain high availability.

Comparisons between Chef and Puppet

Here's a comparison of two configuration management tools—Chef and Puppet, which will enable you to take an informed decision based on the needs and expertise your organisation has in using Chef or Puppet.

	Chef	Puppet
Type	Configuration management, private and public cloud management, DevOps, continuous deployment or delivery	Configuration management, private and public cloud management, DevOps
Licence	Apache licence	Apache from 2.7.0, GPL before that
Language	Ruby (client) and Erlang (server); uses domain-specific language (DSL)	Ruby
Platform support	AIX, *BSD, HP-UX, Linux, Mac OS X, Solaris, Windows *http://docs.getchef.com/install_server.html*	AIX, *BSD, HP-UX, Linux, Mac OS X (partial), Solaris, Windows *https://docs.puppetlabs.com/guides/platforms.html*
Developer base	Growing fast	Huge
Architecture	Chef server, Chef agents, and a Chef workstation for configuration and management	Puppet server and Puppet agents for configuration and management
Agent based	Yes	Yes
Stable release	Ver 11.10.4; February 20, 2014	Ver 3.7.1; September 15, 2014
Community base	Comparatively smaller user base	Large user base
DevOps support	Programmer-friendly approach	Systems admin-friendly approach
Integration with cloud-based platforms	Amazon EC2, VMware, OpenStack, Rackspace, Google Cloud Platform, and Microsoft Azure; it supports automatic provisioning/de-provisioning and configuration of new machines.	Bare metal, VMware, OpenStack, Eucalyptus Cloud, Google Compute Engine, Amazon EC2
Main customers	Facebook, LinkedIn, YouTube, Splunk, Rackspace, GE Capital, Digital Science, Bloomberg	Twitter, Verizon, VMware, Sony, Symantec, Red Hat, Salesforce, Motorola, PayPal
Company	Opscode	Puppet Labs
Documentation	Good	Very Good
Website	*www.getchef.com*	*http://puppetlabs.com*
Documentation	*http://docs.opscode.com/*	*http://docs.puppetlabs.com/*

References

[1] *http://en.wikipedia.org/wiki/Chef_%28software%29*
[2] *http://en.wikipedia.org/wiki/Puppet_%28software%29*
[3] *http://en.wikipedia.org/wiki/Comparison_of_open-source_configuration_management_software*
[4] *http://www.slideshare.net/scriptrock/puppet-vs-chef*
[5] *http://docs.getchef.com/*
[6] *https://www.getchef.com/solutions/aws/*
[7] *https://www.getchef.com/solutions/vmware/*
[8] *https://www.getchef.com/solutions/continuous-delivery/*

By: Priyanka Agashe and Mitesh Soni

Priyanka Agashe is a Software Engineer. She loves to explore new technologies and her professional spheres of interests include Oracle Apps, Electronics, and Robotics.

Mitesh Soni is a Technical Lead in the same organisation. He is in the Cloud Practice and loves to write about new technologies. Blog: *http://clean-clouds.com*

Creating a Basic IP PBX with Asterisk

Asterisk is a software switching platform, capable of running on standardised PC hardware with the requisite accessories to connect to various telecom networks. In this third article in the series, the author explains how to create a basic IP private branch exchange (PBX).

Transforming the open source Asterisk software to a fully functional IP PBX is achieved with a few simple steps. In the previous sessions, we have familiarised ourselves with the general Asterisk environment as well as the common hardware involved. In this article, we will go into the details of creating a basic IP PBX.

We first need to decide on the configuration of the PBX —is it going to be a pure IP PBX or will it also connect to ISDN, GSM, etc? Let's select a very common configuration for the Indian scenario—an IP PBX for 100 subscribers with one PRI and four GSM trunks.

Let us start by defining the OS, which could theoretically be any Linux flavour like Debian, CentOS, Ubuntu, etc. We will base all further discussions on CentOS.

Next is the selection of the hardware. It's preferable to select server hardware rather than typical desktop hardware, as we expect the PBX to run 24 hours and have a lifespan of at least 5-10 years. In a 100-subscriber scenario, we can opt for an Intel dual core or a Core i3 with 4GB RAM and a 500GB hard disk drive. The 100-subscriber configuration can also work with 2GB RAM, but may have quality issues, when a lot of subscribers make calls simultaneously. Even the 4GB RAM set-up may have problems if all the 100 subscribers make calls at the same time. These values are based on my experience of the typical load in a 100-subscriber environment. For higher loads like 500 or 1000 subscribers, the use of higher RAM configurations and SSD hard disks for CDRs and log files is recommended.

After hardware selection and installation of the OS, we move on towards the software installation.

Disabling SELinux

In CentOS, the security-enhanced Linux (SELinux) system is enabled by default, and it often gets in the way of Asterisk. There are multiple articles on the Internet that describe the correct configuration of SELinux, but we'll disable it for the sake of simplicity.

Installing basic libraries

The code given below will install OpenSSL security, the gcc compiler, the ncurses GUI library, the XML library, the SQLite database, etc.

```
yum install -y make wget openssl-devel ncurses-devel newt-
devel libxml2-devel kernel-devel gcc gcc-c++ sqlite-devel
libuuid-devel
```

These base libraries are required for subsequent modules.

Installing DAHDI

DAHDI (Digium/Asterisk Hardware Device Interface) is a framework for interfacing with digital telephony cards in Asterisk. It contains drivers for the interface and also tools for monitoring. As we are using a PRI card in our configuration, this installation needs to be done.

```
Download:
cd /usr/src/
wget http://downloads.asterisk.org/pub/telephony/dahdi-linux-
complete/dahdi-linux-complete-2.9.2+2.9.2.tar.gz
Unzip:
tar zxvf dahdi-linux-complete-2.9.2+2.9.2.tar.gz
Install:
cd /usr/src/dahdi-linux-complete-2.9.2+2.9.2
make
make install
make config
```

Installing *libpri*

libpri is required to handle the protocol part of the PRI interface.

```
Download:
wget http://downloads.asterisk.org/pub/telephony/libpri/
libpri-1.4.15.tar.gz
Unzip:
tar zxvf libpri-1.4.15.tar.gz
Install:
cd /usr/src/libpri-1.4.15.tar.gz
make
make install
```

Installing Asterisk

Now, we are ready to install a basic version of Asterisk. Let's download version 11, which is a LTS (Long Term Support) release.

```
Download:
wget http://downloads.asterisk.org/pub/telephony/asterisk/
releases/asterisk-11.11.0.tar.gz
Unzip:
tar zxvf asterisk-11.11.0.tar.gz
Install:
cd /usr/src/asterisk-11.11.0
./configure
make menuselect
```

Now you get a GUI, a *Menuselect* menu, listing categories such as applications, channel drivers, and PBX modules. On the right-hand side, you'll see a list of modules that correspond with the select category. At the bottom of the screen, you'll see two buttons. You can use the *Tab* key to switch between the various sections, and press the *Enter* key to select or unselect a particular module. If you see [*] next to a module name, it signifies that the module has been selected. If you see *XXX next to a module name, it signifies that the select module cannot be built, as one of its dependencies is missing. In that case, you can look at the bottom of the screen for the line labelled *'Depends upon:'* for a description of the missing dependency. Once *Menuselect* is executed, and the required applications, channel drivers and modules selected, exit the GUI.

```
make
make install
make config
make samples
```

make samples installs the configuration and contains more than just an example configuration. The sample configuration files historically were used predominantly for documentation of available options. As such, they contain many examples for configuring Asterisk that may not be ideal for standard deployments. Sample installation is helpful as it creates sample configurations of all configuration files. We can select specific ones like *sip.conf* and *extensions.conf* and overwrite them. Else, we might need to create a series of configuration files from scratch.

Start services

```
service dahdi start
service asterisk start
```

For Debian or Ubuntu users, the installation of basic libraries and *start* services is slightly different, as shown below:

```
apt-get install build-essential wget libssl-dev libncurses5-
dev libnewt-dev libxml2-dev linux-headers-$(uname -r)
libsqlite3-dev uuid-dev
Start services:
/etc/init.d/dahdi start
/etc/init.d/asterisk start
```

All the other steps remain the same.

Installing SIP phones

Basic Asterisk is an IP PBX, which can interconnect IP phones with the SIP (Session Initiation Protocol) or IAX (Inter Asterisk eXchange) protocol. SIP is quite widespread and best suited for communication with other systems. IAX is a very compact protocol with less bandwidth requirements, which is proprietary to asterisk, and can be used where limited bandwidth is available.

There are three types of endpoints you would typically provide your users with, which could serve as a telephone set. They are popularly referred to as hardphones — physical devices like normal telephones with a handset, buttons, etc; softphones — software applications that run on top of laptops or desktops; and analogue terminal adaptors (ATAs) — connectors for traditional analogue devices like analogue phones, faxes, etc. All of them are configured as SIP extensions in Asterisk. To configure the SIP extensions, we need to edit */etc/asterisk/sip.conf*.

```
[general]
context=unauthenticated
allowguest=no
alwaysauthreject=yes

[test-phone](!)
type=friend
host=dynamic
context=office-device
disallow=all
allow=ulaw
allow=alaw

[ramesh](test-phone)
secret=my5UP3rp@s5!

[suresh](test-phone)

secret=my5UP3rp@s5II
```

The [general] section is a standard section that appears at the top of the configuration file for all channel modules, containing general configuration options for how that protocol relates to your system and can be used to define default parameters as well. In Asterisk, we define all actions based on context. In general, we specify that the default context is the context called 'unauthenticated', with no actions defined in this context. So, if users have not authenticated themselves in a context, they will not be able to carry out any action. The allowguest parameter specifies that any unauthenticated users are not allowed. Unethical hackers try to guess usernames by trying different usernames. By specifying alwaysauthreject, we instruct the system to output 'userrejected' for wrong username+password combinations, and not the 'user not found' message.

In the next section, we define a template we have chosen to name [test-phone]. We've created it as a template so that we can use the values within it for all of our devices.

In the [test-phone] template, we've defined several options required for authentication and control of calls to and from devices that use that template. The first option we've configured is the type, which we've set to friend. This tells the channel driver to attempt to match calls on the name first, and then on the IP address.

The host option is used when we need to send a request to the telephone (such as when we want to call someone). Asterisk needs to know where the device is on the network. By defining the value as dynamic, we let Asterisk know that the telephone will tell us where it is on the network instead of having its location defined statically.

When a request from a telephone is received and authenticated by Asterisk, the requested extension number is handled by the dialplan in the context defined in the device configuration; in our case, the context is named office-device.

The password for the device is defined by the secret parameter. While this is not strictly required, you should note that it is quite common for unethical hackers to run phishing scripts that look for exposed VoIP accounts with insecure passwords and simple device names (such as a device name of 666 with a password of 666). By utilising an uncommon device name such as a MAC address, and a password that is a little harder to guess, we can significantly lower the risk to our system should we need to expose it to the outside world.

Now that we're finished with our template, we can define our device names and, using the test-phone template, greatly simplify the amount of details required under each device section. The device name is defined in the square brackets, and the template to be applied is defined in the parentheses following the device name. We can add additional options to the device name by specifying them below the device name.

Each time we change this file, we need to reload the file at the Asterisk prompt. To start Asterisk in verbose mode, use the following command:

```
asterisk -vvvvr
```

The number of 'v's indicate the level of verbosity required. You will obtain the CLI prompt. To reload SIP configurations, use the following command:

```
*CLI>sip reload
```

You may verify if the new channels are loaded, by typing the following command:

```
*CLI>sip show peers
```

You would have noticed that Suresh and Ramesh do not have any numbers allocated to them. This is done in the dialplan, by editing /etc/asterisk/extensions.conf.

```
[office-device]
exten => 100,1,Dial(SIP/ramesh)
exten => 101,1,Dial(SIP/suresh)
```

This basic dialplan will allow you to dial your SIP devices using extensions 100 and 101. If somebody dials the number 100 in the 'office-device' context, the call will be routed to Ramesh. All of these extensions are arbitrary numbers and could be anything you want. You may also choose 4- or 5-digit numbers. You will need to reload your dialplan before changes take effect in Asterisk.

```
*CLI>diaplan reload
```

You should now be able to dial between your two new extensions. Open up the CLI in order to see the call progression. Before that, you need to set up the new phones with the user name and password defined in sip.conf. It will show something like what follows:

```
Connected to Asterisk 1.8.23.0-vici currently running on
localhost
Versbosity is atleast 21
[Oct 9 18:11:30] == Using SIP RTP CoS mark 5
[Oct 9 18:11:30] -- Executing [100@office-device:1] Dial("SIP/
ramesh-0000005", "SIP/suresh"
[Oct 9 18:11:30] - Called SIP/suresh
[Oct 9 18:11:30] - SIP/suresh-000006 ringing
[Oct 9 18:11:30] - SIP/suresh-000006 answered SIP/ramesh-0000005
[Oct 9 18:11:30] - Locally bridging SIP/ramesh-00000005 and SIP/
suresh-00000006
```

You have made your first successful call between two IP phones. Congratulations! **END**

By: Devasia Kurian

The author is the founder and CEO of *astTECS, an Asterisk software-based company providing IP PBX, call centre dialler, etc. He can be contacted at d.kurian@asttecs.com. Technical queries and support for items described in this article may be addressed to http://www.asttecs.com/asterisk-forum/

Protect Your System Against Shellshock

This informative article explains how the newly discovered Shellshock bug operates. It gives simple, easy-to-implement methods to reduce your system's vulnerability to it as well as minimise the harmful effects.

Shellshock is a security bug, which allows the attacker to execute arbitrary commands in the UNIX bash shell, a command line interface commonly used in UNIX and Linux distributions. This bug was first discovered by Stéphane Chazelas on September 12, 2014, and he initially called it 'bashdoor'. It was assigned the CVE (common vulnerability and exposures) identifier 'CVE-2014-6271', and publicly disclosed on September 24, 2014. This article will discuss the effects of the bug, ways to test your system's vulnerability to it and also explore ways to protect yourself against attackers. Similar vulnerabilities are being discovered continuously and patches are being updated regularly.

Test your system

To test if your system is vulnerable to the Shellshock bug or not, open up a terminal (*Terminal.App* for Mac OS X) and type the following command:

```
env x='() { :;}; echo vulnerable' bash -c 'echo hello'
env x='() { :;}; echo vulnerable' sh -c 'echo hello'
```

Here, we are setting an environment variable 'x'. The part *echo*

vulnerable is the arbitrary command that is being executed before the actual bash command, i.e., *bash -c 'actual command'*, hence giving the attacker a chance to run arbitrary commands on your system.

You can further test your system for the vulnerability (as reported by Tavis Ormandy - CVE-2014-7169) by running the following command:

```
env X='() { (a)=>\' bash -c "echo date"; cat echo
env X='() { (a)=>\' sh -c "echo date"; cat echo
```

You will notice that the date is displayed and you can also find a file named 'echo' in the current directory. This means that your system is still vulnerable.

Here is another test that you can run, which will print out *'not patched'* if your system is not yet patched or is still vulnerable to the bug:

```
env foo='() { echo not patched; }' bash -c foo
```

The widespread effects of Shellshock

The Shellshock bug potentially affects all the systems that

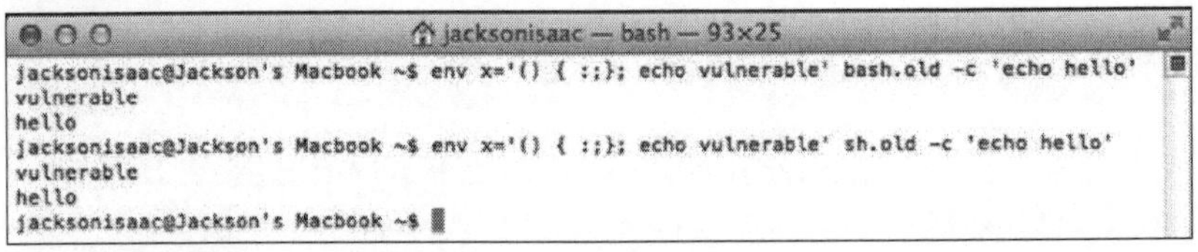

Figure 1: The Shellshock vulnerability test

have bash running on them. Bash is installed as the system's default command line interface on many Linux and UNIX-based systems including Mac OS X. Based on the source code analysis of bash, about *25 years' worth of bash versions* since the early 1990s through version 4.3 (in Linux systems) and version 3.2.48 (in Mac OS X) seem to be vulnerable. The vulnerability might exist beyond these versions as well, based on recent reports about the patches not being entirely effective.

It would be very difficult to patch all the systems that are affected by this bug, as bash is used in almost all devices like modems, home routers, Internet of Things (IoT) with embedded Linux, Web servers and devices connected to the Internet. Although bash is not directly exposed to the Internet, software or an application that is connected to the Internet can be used to run commands through bash internally on the vulnerable systems.

Operating systems that bash supports allow environment variables to be set, which are dynamic in nature. The attacker can attach some malicious code to this environment variable that will be executed once the variable is received. The attacker can force an application to send this specially crafted environment variable to bash, and it could be used to create a self-replicating worm.

According to a survey by Netcraft, we can conclude that almost half the online servers are running on Apache, which in turn runs on Linux machines and would have bash installed. As a result of this, half the Internet is vulnerable to the Shellshock bug.

The most likely method to attack systems is through Web servers using CGI (Common Gateway Interface), which is widely used to generate dynamic Web content. CGI scripts can be used to execute bash commands without the need for any authentication.

The bash continues processing commands after the function definition, resulting in what is generally termed as 'code injection attack'. The problem is that the auto-import function parser runs past the end of the function definition and keeps executing the codes. An attacker can gain access through this, and can then compromise and infect other systems on the network. FreeBSD and NetBSD have disabled auto import functions in bash version 3.2.54 onwards, by default, to prevent future vulnerabilities.

According to Wikipedia, the security firm Incapsula noted 17,400 attacks on more than 1,800 Web domains, originating from 400 unique IP addresses on September 26, 2014; 55 per cent of the attacks originated from China and the United States. By September 30, the website performance firm CloudFlare said it was tracking approximately 1.5 million attacks and

probes per day related to the Shellshock bug.

Updating bash

In order to reduce your system's vulnerability to Shellshock, you can update bash in the OS you are using. Here's how you can do so.

Build bash from source on Mac OS X

Here I'll show you how to rebuild bash from source on Mac OS X, as the patch released by Apple Inc is not entirely effective against some of the vulnerabilities.

> **Note:** Make sure your Mac has *Xcode* and *Xcode command line* tools installed.

Open up *Terminal.App* and type in the following commands.
(i) To download the bash tarball and apply patches:

```
$ curl https://opensource.apple.com/tarballs/bash/bash-92.
tar.gz | tar zxf -

$ cd bash-92/bash-3.2

$ curl https://ftp.gnu.org/pub/gnu/bash/bash-3.2-patches/
bash32-052 | patch -p0

$ curl https://ftp.gnu.org/pub/gnu/bash/bash-3.2-patches/
bash32-053 | patch -p0

$ curl https://ftp.gnu.org/pub/gnu/bash/bash-3.2-patches/
bash32-054 | patch -p0

$ curl https://ftp.gnu.org/pub/gnu/bash/bash-3.2-patches/
bash32-055 | patch -p0

$ curl https://ftp.gnu.org/pub/gnu/bash/bash-3.2-patches/
bash32-056 | patch -p0

$ curl https://ftp.gnu.org/pub/gnu/bash/bash-3.2-patches/
bash32-057 | patch -p0
```

Here, we need to add patches starting from 052 and apply the later patches subsequently.

> **Note:** Bash 3.2 patches 52, 53, and 54 correspond to Bash 4.3 patches 25, 26, 27 and so on.

(ii) Rebuild bash: After applying the patches in the bash-3.2 folder, we move up to the bash-92 folder and build the source:

```
$ cd ..
$ xcodebuild
```

(iii) Back up and update default bash: Now let us check the version of the bash we have built, take a back-up of the old bash, and replace the latter with the built version of bash.

```
$ build/Release/bash  version
```

```
$ build/Release/sh --version
```

```
$ sudo cp /bin/bash /bin/bash.backup
```

```
$ sudo cp /bin/bash /bin/sh.backup
```

```
$ sudo cp build/Release/bash /bin
```

```
$ sudo cp build/Release/sh /bin
```

You can also add a *chmod a-x* to the backed-up version to prevent it from being used, instead of the newer version:

```
$ sudo chmod a-x /bin/bash.backup
```

```
$ sudo chmod a-x /bin/sh.backup
```

Update bash on Debian-based systems (Ubuntu, etc)

Ubuntu/Debian users can easily update bash through the official repositories with the help of 'apt-get':

```
$ sudo apt-get update
```

```
$ sudo apt-get install bash
```

You can also run the following command in a terminal:

```
$ sudo apt-get -only-upgrade install bash
```

Update bash on Fedora systems

Type the following command to update bash on Fedora systems:

```
$ sudo yum update bash
```

References

[1] http://en.wikipedia.org/wiki/Shellshock_(software_bug)
[2] http://apple.stackexchange.com/questions/146849/how-do-i-recompile-bash-to-avoid-shellshock-the-remote-exploit-cve-2014-6271-an
[3] http://www.lynda.com/articles/shellshock-bash-exploit
[4] http://www.troyhunt.com/2014/09/everything-you-need-to-know-about.html
[5] http://www.symantec.com/connect/blogs/shellshock-all-you-need-know-about-bash-bug-vulnerability
[6] http://news.netcraft.com/archives/2014/09/24/september-2014-web-server-survey.html

By: Jackson Isaac

The author is an active open source contributor to projects like GNOME-Music, Mozilla Firefox and Mozillians. You can follow him on *jacksonisaac.wordpress.com* or reach him by mail at *jacksonisaac2008@gmail.com*

OSFY Magazine Attractions During 2014-15

MONTH	THEME	FEATURED LIST	BUYERS' GUIDE
March 2014	Network monitoring	Security	-------------------
April 2014	Android Special	Anti Virus	Wifi Hotspot Devices
May 2014	Backup and Data Storage	Certification	External Storage
June 2014	Open Source on Windows	Mobile Apps	UTMs fo SMEs
July 2014	Firewall and Network security	Web Hosting Solutions Providers	MFD Printers for SMEs
August 2014	Kernel Development	Big Data Solutions Providers	SSDs for Servers
September 2014	Open Source for Start-ups	Cloud	Android Devices
October 2014	Mobile App Development	Training on Programming Languages	Projectors
November 2014	Cloud Special	Virtualisation Solutions Providers	Network Switches and Routers
December 2014	Web Development	Leading Ecommerce Sites	AV Conferencing
January 2015	Programming Languages	IT Consultancy Service Providers	Laser Printers for SMEs
February 2015	Top 10 of Everything on Open Source	Storage Solutions Providers	Wireless Routers

Decrypt https Traffic with Wireshark

In this article, the author demystifies the business of encrypting and decrypting network traffic, and translates arcane terms such as https, ssh, sftp, etc.

Wireshark, an interesting open source network sniffer, can not only read network traffic, but can further decrypt https traffic provided you have the private key! Let's learn more about decrypting https traffic using this tool.

To keep a network traffic sniffer from revealing login credentials, secure protocols such as https, ssh, sftp, etc, are used instead of their respective clear text protocols like http, telnet and ftp. Secure protocols encrypt traffic travelling between two end points; thus all the traffic available on the network is unreadable unless and until decrypted.

To understand secure protocols, let me try to explain the basics of encryption and decryption in simple terms.

Encryption and decryption

Encryption is a technique used to make readable (clear text) data unreadable (cipher text), typically using complex mathematical algorithms. Decryption is the exact reverse of the process of encryption.

The two main types of encryption

Symmetric key encryption: A single key is used to encrypt and to decrypt. Examples of the symmetric key algorithm are the advance encryption standard (AES), data encryption standard (DES), etc. The typical length of a key is 128 bytes onwards, making encryption-decryption fast. However, the key must be known to both sides for successful operation.

Asymmetric key encryption: A key pair is used for encryption and decryption. Text encrypted by one key can be decrypted only by the second key and vice versa. Thus, the same key cannot perform encryption and its corresponding decryption. Examples of the asymmetric key encryption algorithm are Rivest, Shamir Adleman (RSA), ElGamal, Elliptic curve cryptography, etc.

Some important points about asymmetric key encryption are:

1. Asymmetric key encryption and decryption is slow compared to symmetric key encryption. For example, RSA encryption with a 1024-bit key is about 250 times slower compared to AES encryption with a 128-bit key.
2. One key (a private key) is kept confidential and the other key (the public one) is distributed.
3. Text encrypted by the sender's private key can be decrypted by the sender's public key. Thus, practically anybody can decrypt this since this key is distributed. However, please note that this ensures the authenticity of the sender—the private key is held confidential by

the corresponding sender.

4. Text encrypted by a receiver's public key can be decrypted only by the receiver's private key; thus messages encrypted using the public key of the receiver can be decrypted only by the corresponding receiver with the corresponding private key. The https protocol uses this feature.

Figure 1: SSL decryption properties

The https protocol

As discussed in earlier Wireshark articles, it is definitely possible to sniff (eavesdrop) network traffic leading to compromise of sensitive information such as login names, passwords, etc. If clear text protocol is in use. The https protocol is used to guard against possibility of clear text information between client (browser) and server getting compromised.

The https protocol uses the secure socket layer (SSL) or its successor, the transport layer security (TLS) to encrypt traffic between the Web server and the client (browser). SSL, in turn, uses an asymmetric key RSA algorithm for encryption and decryption. When a user sends a browser request to an https website, encrypted communication is established as follows:

1. The browser sends an https request for a secure session towards the server's TCP 443 port (or on a different port for servers running on non-standard ports).
2. The server sends back its digital certificate – which contains its public key.
3. The browser authenticates this certificate with the certifying authority (CA) – the provider of the digital certificate, before continuing further. If the certificate is not authenticated by the CA or self generated, an error like 'This connection is untrusted' is received. This could be a man-in-the-middle (MITM) type of attack, where the attacker makes two independent connections – one with the user and the other with the server, to capture the complete traffic in decrypted format. The user should abort such a connection, or may proceed further only if the origin of the certificate is assured.
4. The client generates a random sequence of characters to be used as a symmetric key.
5. The client encrypts these characters using the server's public key and sends it to the server, thus ensuring that only the corresponding server (or private key) can decrypt it.
6. The server decrypts the symmetric key using its private key.
7. Now, this set of characters is known only to the client and the server. They are used as the symmetric key for

encrypting all further traffic between client and server.
8. The client and the server start encrypted communication using this symmetric key.

You may wonder about the jugglery involved in using a 'hybrid' technique. This is done merely to improve speed since the symmetric key provides much faster encryption and decryption.

> ### Box 1: The importance of the private key and the criticality of Heartbleed
>
> The private key of the server is held confidentially on the server side. So it is obvious that if this key is compromised, it could be used to decrypt sensitive data between the server and the client. It is a primary requirement that this private key is really held privately!
>
> The most popularly used open source software for SSL and TLS is OpenSSL–which was first released in 1998.
>
> Heartbleed could reveal the private key of the server by exploiting a serious vulnerability in OpenSSL. Thus, its arrival was a nightmare for security professionals.

Now, we have sufficient information to understand the capturing and decrypting of https traffic using Wireshark. Start Wireshark and browse any https website–you will definitely notice that the data part of the capture is encrypted. To decrypt data, we must have the private key of the https server.

So, let us proceed with the following steps. This article uses VMware ESXi 5.0 as the target system to decrypt https traffic using Wireshark.

A. Enable VMware SSH:
▪ Use the VMware console keyboard
▪ Press the F2 key
▪ Provide your login credentials
▪ Select troubleshooting options
▪ Enable ESXi shellB.
B. Copy the private key file using the SSH command:

```
ssh root@vmwareesxi:/etc/vmware/ssl/rui.key .
```

C. Start Wireshark, and let traffic capture begin – you may use capture filter for the VMware ESXi host.
D. Open the browser, then open the VMware ESXi https Web page and browse a few links.
E. Capture traffic and stop.
F. Now, apply the private key to the SSL traffic from this host (as shown in Figure 1):
▪ Edit – Preferences
▪ Protocols
▪ SSL
▪ RSA keys list: Edit
▪ Insert the required values: IP address, port number, protocol and key file path+name
▪ Textbox2 – RSA private key format – RSA key does not require password. The password field is for the file in the PKCS#12 format.

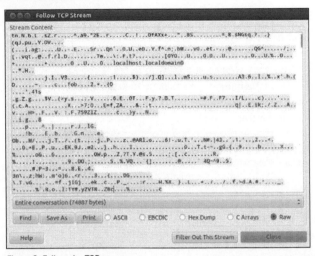

Figure 2: Follow the TCP stream

Box 2: Format of the RSA private key

```
-----BEGIN RSA PRIVATE KEY-----
MAIEpAIBAAKCAQEAxcVEgXm4nNIseFneHmWIOO/qx-
aQnhZ/FxB4RmWW9DXRuhU6P
YtdMI2O3C4z5W6t7JyLpTsCJ1egWE5CSIyRY37ncs
qJsu8WQ6CsIfPlEERmQVh4K92bryK
.
.
WGcsadfrG/rWcpYpiNfsGBu0Qd25ZwirepLOcBobX
UMXaQ1JoG0AokLEoVECCtTnDaKh
HEJ4yX4GsdfHfseSdsf9sdfhf9In0DBRjo0J3ttJdAPO
MwqCMfK4CCfB2F4eQcwhg==
-----END RSA PRIVATE KEY-----
```

G. Start the browser and open *https://vmwareesxi*
  - Right-click any packet and look at what's shown under 'Follow TCP stream' – this will show the encrypted https traffic as seen in Figure 2.
  - Use 'Follow SSL stream' to view the traffic in the decrypted format as depicted in Figure 3.

If all the steps are followed correctly, the captured traffic will be seen in a decrypted format.

Protecting against https RSA decryption

This decryption method is successful only if RSA is used to encrypt and decrypt the symmetric key – which is sent across from the client to the server via the network (in encrypted form). So is there a way out? Yes, definitely.

The Diffie Hellman (DH) key exchange method plays a vital role in ensuring the security of https. DH creates a shared secret between two systems without actually transmitting the 'encryption key' across the wire. However, DH is only a key exchange method; it does not authenticate the server nor does it encrypt the data.

By combining RSA, which provides server authentication and DH (which enables the creation of a shared encryption key at the client and the server ends), the result is excellent protection against https decryption even if a private key is available.

RSA and DH in combination are used by various open source distros such as IPCop and OpenFiler, thus making sure that a compromised private key is not sufficient for successful decryption.

Diagnosing decryption related issues

1. Make sure that you capture all the traffic right from the first packet in order to enable decryption. A point to ponder over is that the encryption key is transmitted in encrypted format between client and server before the actual data transfer. If you miss this traffic, the key will not be available and further decryption will not be possible.
2. Use Wireshark decryption logs, which can be enabled by specifying the log file name under *Edit – Preferences – Protocols – SSL – (Pre)-Master-Secret*. This file can then be checked to find the decryption status. Please see Box 3 and Box 4 for unsuccessful and successful decryption logs.

Box 3: Unsuccessful decryption

dissect_ssl enter frame #23 (first time) conversation = 0x7fda095a1d18, ssl_session = 0x7fda095a21c8
record: offset = 0, reported_length_remaining = 1091
dissect_ssl3_record found version 0x0301 -> state 0x11
dissect_ssl3_record: content_type 22
decrypt_ssl3_record: app_data len 49, ssl state 0x11
packet_from_server: is from server - TRUE
decrypt_ssl3_record: using server decoder
decrypt_ssl3_record: no decoder available
dissect_ssl3_handshake iteration 1 type 2 offset 5 length 45 bytes, remaining 54
dissect_ssl3_hnd_hello_common found SERVER RANDOM -> state 0x13
ssl_restore_session can't find stored session
dissect_ssl3_hnd_srv_hello found CIPHER 0x0035 -> state 0x17
dissect_ssl3_hnd_srv_hello trying to generate keys
ssl_generate_keyring_material not enough data to generate key (0x17 required 0x37 or 0x57)
Please use this text in bold or as a footer for Box 3.

Box 4: Successful decryption

ssl_association_remove removing TCP 443 - http handle 0x7fd2ef884150
Private key imported: KeyID bc:8f:2c:fc:c2:54:67:f7:cc:0a :1c:34:21:b3:80:9e:...
ssl_init IPv4 addr '192.168.51.2' (192.168.51.2)
port '443' filename '/home/rajesh/Desktop/rui.key' password(only for p12 file) ''
ssl_init private key file /home/rajesh/Desktop/rui.key successfully loaded.
association_add TCP port 443 protocol http handle 0x7fd2ef884150

In this article, I have tried to describe various encryption

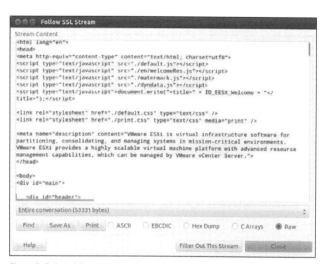

Figure 3: Follow SSL stream

A word of caution

Packets captured using the test scenarios described in this series of articles are capable of revealing sensitive information such as login names and passwords. Using ARP spoofing, in particular, will disturb the network temporarily. Make sure to use these techniques only in a test environment. If at all you wish to use them in a live environment, do not forget to avail explicit written permission before doing so.

techniques, DH and RSA only to enable a basic understanding of the topics. For those who want to know more, please search the Web, especially Wikipedia.

An interesting note: Websites using the https protocol are called 'secure' websites only to the extent that the communication between browser and Web server is encrypted and, further, the server is authenticated by CA – but nothing beyond that! It does not guarantee that the Web applications or the site is secure enough. END

References

[1] DH with RSA: *http://security.stackexchange.com/questions/35471/is-there-any-particular-reason-to-use-diffie-hellman-over-rsa-for-key-exchange*

[2] One of the commercial products affected by Heartbleed was VMware ESXi (versions 5.0, 5.1 and 5.5) – its security update was released immediately. Read VMware's advisory for Heartbleed at: *http://www.vmware.com/security/advisories/VMSA-2014-0006.html*

[3] OpenSSL Heartbleed security notice and update instructions for Ubuntu: *http://www.ubuntu.com/usn/usn-2165-1/*

By: Rajesh Deodhar

The author is an IS auditor, network security consultant and trainer. He is an industrial electronics engineer with CISA, CISSP and DCL certifications. Please feel free to contact him on *rajesh at omegasystems dot co dot in*

Install and Configure Git on CentOS 7

This article explains to beginners and intermediate Linux users how to install, configure and use Git. It's also for those who are comfortable with Linux but are hesitant to use Git, due to their lack of familiarity with it.

Git is a distributed version control system (DVCS) created by Linus Torvalds. It's mostly used by developers, but it can also be used to store your dot files (a dot file begins with a '.' and the term is generally used to refer to *.bashrc*, *.vimrc* or other such set-up/configuration files), important scripts, etc.

It's different from other similar DVCS systems because it does not treat data as a set of files, but rather, when you save your project in Git, it takes a snapshot of how the files look at that instant in time and stores a reference to it. The core of Git is a key-value data system. No matter what data you insert into Git, it will checksum it using an *SHA 1* algorithm and create a 40-character hex key. Therefore, the name of the file is not really relevant to Git.

GitHub is a Web-based hosting service; it offers a remote Git repository where you can host your files.

> **Note:** You don't need GitHub to use Git. You can host your remote repository on a company server as well.

Git terminology

Let's get familiar with some terminology:

- *Working tree:* This is the directory in which you put the files that you want Git to manage. This is where you store files so that they can be staged to be pushed into the repository. Basically, this could be any directory on your local file system that has a Git repository associated with it. When you run the *git init* command in a normal directory, it transforms the normal directory into a working tree (working directory), because running that command creates a *.git* sub-directory right inside the directory in which you have run the command. We'll soon see how this is done.

- *Repository (Git directory):* The repository, also called the Git directory, is where all your game-changing Git files are stored and where all the Git goodness starts. It basically stores all the meta data, objects, etc, for your project.

  - A local repository exists on your laptop and is associated with your working tree. It's the *.git* directory that gets created when you run *git init* as stated earlier.

- A remote repository exists outside of your laptop, somewhere on a remote server. In our case, it will be on GitHub.
- *Git objects:* There are different kinds of objects that Git uses such as:
  - Tree–This contains one or more 'trees' and blobs. A tree is a sort of a file system directory and it can point to other Git trees. Think of it as a directory having other sub-directories or 'blobs'.
  - Blobs–These are just normal plain files such as text files, source code files, or even pictures; something like the file contents or the *inode* information. Basically, a blob can be thought of as something that's not a directory.
  - Commit–This is generated the moment you run the *git commit* command. It has the meta data as well as a pointer to the root project directory, so that the snap shots can be recreated whenever needed.
- *Git index:* This is the staging area of Git. When you run the *git add* command, you add files to this staging area. When you run the *git commit* command, these files are committed to your local Git database. You then push the files into the remote repository.

> **Note:** The index is NOT the repository, neither is it the working tree/directory.

- *Git commit:* This is a point in time snapshot of your working directory. You run the *git commit* command and the files are committed to the local Git database as stated earlier. This command basically checksums all the files and directories in the location where it is run and creates a commit object.
- *Branch:* It is a pointer to a commit. The default branch name in Git is 'master'. The master branch appears the first time we do a commit. If we do another commit, the master then points to this new commit.

There is other terminology, but this is enough for starters.

Opening a GitHub account

So let's open a GitHub account first. Head to *www.github.com* and sign up. It's free.

> **Note:** Please note down the e-mail address and the password you use to create this account. We will need it in a while when we configure Git on the laptop or desktop.

Once registration is complete, you can sign in. On the top right side of the page, you will see the name you chose and there will be a '+' sign next to it. Click on it and then on the new repository option. Take a look at the screenshot in Figure 1.

On the next page, choose any name for your repository. Mine's called *mydotfiles*. Provide a brief description about your repository. Please do not select the 'Initialise this repository with a README' option because we will be

Figure 1: Create repo

Figure 2: Git repo

creating a README ourselves.

Click on the 'Create repository' button and when the next page loads, make a note of the URL shown.

Figure 3 shows how it looks in my case. This is a screenshot of the top half of the page that loads up when you hit the 'Create repository' button showing the Git remote repository name.

Important note: Please remember, whatever repository name you choose, you'll either need to have a directory with exactly the same name or, you'll need to create a new directory with the same name. Git is basically used to sync your directories and files located inside a directory on your laptop with the one having the same name on GitHub.

Installing and configuring Git for first time use

Install Git by running:

```
yum install git
```

Once you have it installed, run the *git –version* command to see which version we are on. This is how it looks on my laptop:

```
[pmu@t430 ~]$ git --version
git version 1.8.3.1
[pmu@t430 ~]$
```

Now, let's configure Git for first time use. We will set up the name and e-mail address on our local laptop or desktop. This is the step we have to run the very first time we set up Git on a laptop or desktop.

Figure 3: Git remote address

Important: Please ensure that you use the same e-mail ID that you used to create the GitHub account.

```
[pmu@t430 ~]$ git config --global user.name "pmu"
[pmu@t430 ~]$ git config --global user.email "pmu.rwx@gmail.
com"
```

Check the Git man page to see what other options can be set. Once done, you can check the options with the following command:

```
[pmu@t430 ~]$ git config --list
```

Initialising Git

We will now create a directory with the same name as that of the repository.

```
[pmu@t430 ~]$ mkdir mydotfiles
```

Let's get into the directory and initialise Git by running the *git init* command. Once you do that, there should be a *.git* directory created in there with a few files and directories under it. In Git terminology, the *mydotfiles* directory has now become a working tree. Now, the *mydotfiles* directory and everything under it can be uploaded to Git.

Creating files for some Git action

We will create the Readme file now and add some content to it. I created a *Readme.txt* file in Vim, saved it and then ran the *more* command to show the output in the terminal.

```
[pmu@t430 mydotfiles]$ vim Readme.txt
[pmu@t430 mydotfiles]$ more Readme.txt
```

This is a Readme file, my first file that I'll try to upload on GitHub.

```
[pmu@t430 mydotfiles]$
```

You can add anything you want to the file.

Now let's run the *git status* command. This is a very helpful command that lets us know exactly what stage we are at.

Now let's look at the concept that's unique to Git. The moment we add a file, Git creates a hash checksum and refers to the file using that checksum. In other words, we call the file *Readme.txt* but Git refers to it by its checksum. If we were to look for files in a directory, we'd run the *ls* command. With Git, we run the Git *ls-files --stage* command.

```
[pmu@t430 mydotfiles]$ git ls-files --stage
100644 b70f72952f495b2aae83f2ff1a50b5ee8d001edb 0 Readme.txt
[pmu@t430 mydotfiles]$
```

Look at the long string -

b70f72952f495b2aae83f2ff1a50b5ee8d001edb. That's how Git refers to what we call the *Readme.txt* file. So what does this file have? Well, we could check it as follows:

```
[pmu@t430 mydotfiles]$ git show b70f
```

This is a Readme file, my first file that I'll try to upload on GitHub.

```
[pmu@t430 mydotfiles]$
```

That's the Git equivalent of more *Readme.txt* or *cat Readme.txt*. That's exactly the same content we have in our *Readme.txt* file. Note that we can just supply the first four characters of the hash. So this means that Git really doesn't track or manage a file using the filename we give to it. It just 'cares about' the hashed checksum. In other words, if two or more files were to have the exact same content, then the hash checksum generated for those files will be exactly the same.

The following example will make it even clearer.

Let's copy the *Readme.txt* file with some other name without changing any content inside the actual file.

```
[pmu@t430 mydotfiles]$ cp Readme.txt Oncemore.txt

[pmu@t430 mydotfiles]$ ls -l
total 8
-rw-rw-r--. 1 pmu pmu 72 Sep 22 21:03 Oncemore.txt
-rw-rw-r--. 1 pmu pmu 72 Sep 22 20:53 Readme.txt

[pmu@t430 mydotfiles]$
```

Let's run the Git status command and see how it responds.

```
[pmu@t430 mydotfiles]$ git status
# On branch master
# Initial commit
# Changes to be committed:
#   (use "git rm --cached <file>..." to unstage)
#     new file:   Readme.txt
# Untracked files:
#   (use "git add <file>..." to include in what will be
committed)
#     Oncemore.txt
[pmu@t430 mydotfiles]$
```

It shows the newly created file. Note that it states *Readme.txt* as a new file, because we just added it with the *git add Readme.txt* command. We also have a copy of that file with the name *Oncemore.txt*. Since we have still not added it, it shows up as an untracked file.

Will Git show some different output with the Git *ls-files --stage* command this time?

```
[pmu@t430 mydotfiles]$ git ls-files --stage
100644 b70f72952f495b2aae83f2ff1a50b5ee8d001edb 0    Readme.
txt
[pmu@t430 mydotfiles]$
```

No, it does not. So, let's go ahead and add the *Oncemore.txt* file. We will use a '.' this time so that it adds all the files *(Readme.txt* and *Oncemore.txt)*.

```
[pmu@t430 mydotfiles]$ git add .

[pmu@t430 mydotfiles]$ git status
# On branch master
# Initial commit
# Changes to be committed:
#   (use "git rm --cached <file>..." to unstage)
#     new file:   Oncemore.txt
#     new file:   Readme.txt
[pmu@t430 mydotfiles]$
```

Note how the *Oncemore.txt* file now shows up as a new file instead of as 'untracked'. So, how does Git see these two files? Let's find out again with the Git *ls-files –stage* command.

```
[pmu@t430 mydotfiles]$ git ls-files --stage
100644 b70f72952f495b2aae83f2ff1a50b5ee8d001edb 0    Oncemore.
txt
100644 b70f72952f495b2aae83f2ff1a50b5ee8d001edb 0    Readme.
txt
[pmu@t430 mydotfiles]$
```

Well, it's basically two files with different names, but with the same checksum.

The following output confirms it:

```
[pmu@t430 mydotfiles]$ git ls-files --stage | awk {'print $2'}
| sort | uniq
b70f72952f495b2aae83f2ff1a50b5ee8d001edb
[pmu@t430 mydotfiles]$
```

Indeed, the checksum value is the same; it's just that there are two file names associated with it. The *git show* command lets us peek into the file using the checksum value. If you and I were to see the file content, we would use *cat/more/less* or something like that. But Git uses the *git show* command and we supply the checksum to it.

```
[pmu@t430 mydotfiles]$ git show b70f
This is a Readme file, my first file that I'll try to upload on
GitHub.
[pmu@t430 mydotfiles]$
```

If you were expecting to see the content mentioned twice, you're still thinking the 'filename

way' which is not the case here. For Git, it's just b70f72952f495b2aae83f2ff1a50b5ee8d001edb. This is what Git calls a blob.

Let's leave *Oncemore.txt* alone for a while now and just focus on *Readme.txt*.

We'll now run the *git commit* command, which will add the file to the Git local repository.

```
@t430 mydotfiles]$ git commit -m "Adding my first file - Readme.
txt" Readme.txt
[master (root-commit) 26ab994] Adding my first file - Readme.
txt
 1 file changed, 1 insertion(+)
 create mode 100644 Readme.txt
[pmu@t430 mydotfiles]$
```

The output shows that the *Readme.txt* file is now committed to the repository. The part added in quotes after *-m* is the message or comment. The output above tells us that there is one insertion and the last three digits that appear after the 'create mode' word – 644 indicate the 'umask' of the file. So what's the number 26ab994? Let's find out using the *git show* command once again:

```
[pmu@t430 mydotfiles]$ git show 26ab994
commit 26ab994663499b21d8e2de7fc0f53925954fae7c
Author: pmu <pmu.rwx@gmail.com>
Date:   Mon Sep 22 21:08:18 2014 +0530
    Adding my first file - Readme.txt
diff --git a/Readme.txt b/Readme.txt
new file mode 100644
index 0000000..b70f729
--- /dev/null
+++ b/Readme.txt
@@ -0,0 +1 @@
+This is a Readme file, my first file that I'll try to upload on
GitHub.
[pmu@t430 mydotfiles]$
```

That is the commit object hash checksum. This is the Git object which has the author's name, the date and time, the comment, the hashed checksum name of the file that was committed, and some more information. Note that in the line 'index 0000000..b70f729', the last seven digits are nothing but the first seven digits of the checksum that Git created for our *Readme.txt* file.

Let's run the *git status* command again.

```
[pmu@t430 mydotfiles]$ git status
# On branch master
# Changes to be committed:
#   (use "git reset HEAD <file>..." to unstage)
#     new file:   Oncemore.txt
[pmu@t430 mydotfiles]$
```

This makes sense, because we committed only the *Readme.txt* file, but didn't commit the *Oncemore.txt* file. Git's telling us the same. It's telling us that we still have not committed the *Oncemore.txt* file.

Pushing to GitHub

Now, it's time to push our *Readme.txt* file onto GitHub, which is our remote repository. Well, first let's check if we have any remote repository already residing in there.

```
[pmu@t430 mydotfiles]$ git remote -v
[pmu@t430 mydotfiles]$
```

No, we don't have it. So let's go ahead and add the remote repository. Do you remember that in the beginning of the tutorial, we had noted down the repository URL? That's the one we will use. The command for that is *git remote add origin the_name_of_your_github_repo.git*.

In my case it will look like what follows:

```
[pmu@t430 mydotfiles]$ git remote add origin https://github.
com/ugrankar/mydotfiles.git
```

Let's see what the *git remote -v* command says this time.

```
[pmu@t430 mydotfiles]$ git remote -v
origin https://github.com/ugrankar/mydotfiles.git (fetch)
origin https://github.com/ugrankar/mydotfiles.git (push)
[pmu@t430 mydotfiles]$
```

It shows the repository added.
Here's what the command means.
- *git remote add:* This means 'add the remote directory to Git'.
- *origin:* This is the default name for the remote location, so that you can use it instead of typing the lengthy *https://github.com/ugrankar/mydotfiles.git* line. I could have used the word 'pmu' instead of 'origin' or even 'abracadabra' instead of 'origin'. It doesn't matter. But 'origin' seems to be the name that's used most often and, as mentioned before, it's the default name. So we will use that.

Before we run the next command, open up your GitHub repository in your browser.

Figure 4 shows how mine looks.

Now, let's push the file to GitHub using the *git push origin master* command.

```
[pmu@t430 mydotfiles]$ git push origin master
```

> **Note:** You'll have to use the same username and password that you use to create and access your GitHub account. There's a method to add ssh keys, but let's go this way for starters.

Refresh the GitHub page and you'll see your *Readme.txt*

file there. Note the line that says 'latest commit 26ab994663' which is the commit object.

Let's get back to the output captured above.

Note the line where it mentions 'counting objects' and 'Total 3 (delta 0)'. It's '3 Object' in there. So what are these objects?

Git has a command *git rev-list –objects –all* that will list out all the objects.

```
[pmu@t430 mydotfiles]$ git rev-list --objects --all
```

The *got rev-list –objects –all* command shows all the objects.
So let's check them one by one using the 'git show' command.

```
[pmu@t430 mydotfiles]$ git show 26ab
commit 26ab994663499b21d8e2de7fc0f53925954fae7c
Author: pmu <pmu.rwx@gmail.com>
Date:   Mon Sep 22 21:08:18 2014 +0530
    Adding my first file - Readme.txt
diff --git a/Readme.txt b/Readme.txt
new file mode 100644
index 0000000..b70f729
--- /dev/null
+++ b/Readme.txt
@@ -0,0 +1 @@
+This is a Readme file, my first file that I'll try to upload on
GitHub.
[pmu@t430 mydotfiles]$
```

So that's the commit object.
Let's check more:

```
[pmu@t430 mydotfiles]$ git show 82b77
tree 82b77

Readme.txt
```

That's the tree, or the working tree, as Git would refer to it, and *mydotfiles*, as how I would call it.

And now for the next entry:

```
[pmu@t430 mydotfiles]$ git show b70f
This is a Readme file, my first file that I'll try to upload on
GitHub.
[pmu@t430 mydotfiles]$
```

That's our *Readme.txt* file.

> **Note:** Git says it's just got the *Readme.txt* file in it. But we also had the *Oncemore.txt* file in there, didn't we? Yes, we did, but we had just 'added' the file, not committed it.

So let's commit the *Oncemore.txt* file and see what we get:

```
[pmu@t430 mydotfiles]$ git commit -m "Now adding the Oncemore.
txt file" Oncemore.txt
[master 2aa51b8] Now adding the Oncemore.txt file
 1 file changed, 1 insertion(+)
 create mode 100644 Oncemore.txt
[pmu@t430 mydotfiles]$
```

Run the *git status* command like the last time.

```
[pmu@t430 mydotfiles]$ git status
# On branch master
nothing to commit, working directory clean
[pmu@t430 mydotfiles]$
```

The output states that we have nothing to commit. Let's check the objects we have:

```
[pmu@t430 mydotfiles]$ git rev-list --objects --all
```

There are now five objects. The first and the third in the list above seem to be new, so let's check them out.

```
[pmu@t430 mydotfiles]$ git show 2aa5
commit 2aa51b8cae195fb0d786115898179b20b51a094b
Author: pmu <pmu.rwx@gmail.com>
Date:   Mon Sep 22 21:20:26 2014 +0530

    Now adding the Oncemore.txt file

diff --git a/Oncemore.txt b/Oncemore.txt
new file mode 100644
index 0000000..b70f729
--- /dev/null
+++ b/Oncemore.txt
@@ -0,0 +1 @@
+This is a Readme file, my first file that I'll try to upload on
GitHub.
[pmu@t430 mydotfiles]$


[pmu@t430 mydotfiles]$ git show 6116
tree 6116

Oncemore.txt
Readme.txt
[pmu@t430 mydotfiles]$
```

Note that 2aa5 is the commit object created after we ran the *git commit* command for *Oncemore.txt* and 6116 is the working tree object, which now shows two files – *Readme.txt* and *Oncemore.txt*.

Note that the checksum starting with b70f is now associated with the *Oncemore.txt* file.

We can do a *git push* using the below command.

```
[pmu@t430 mydotfiles]$ git push origin master
```

Figure 4: Before *push*

Figure 5: After *push*

Take a look at your GitHub page and it should show you that it's uploaded. Figure 6 shows how my page looks now.

Note how the comment for *Oncemore.txt* is the same as it was for the *Readme.txt*. We had committed *Oncemore.txt* with the comment, 'Now adding the *Oncemore.txt* file'; so why did Git retain the same comment that we used while committing *Oncremore.txt*? Once again, for Git, the file name does not matter. It sees that the commit is for the same Blob and hence retains the command.

This time, it uploads two objects—the commit object (for *Oncemore.txt*) and the working tree object. Why the working tree object again? That's because the working tree object gets a new checksum after we added the *Oncemore.txt* file to it. Run the *git show* command with the four-character hex and you'll see what I mean.

Now, let's try to change the content of *Oncemore.txt* file and see what happens.

I've added a line so that the *Oncemore.txt* file looks like what follows:

```
[pmu@t430 mydotfiles]$ more Oncemore.txt
This is a Readme file, my first file that I'll try to upload on
GitHub.
This is a new line added to the Oncemore.txt file. It's not
there in the Readme.txt file.
[pmu@t430 mydotfiles]$
```

Let's run *git status* and see what it tells us:

```
[pmu@t430 mydotfiles]$ git status
```

```
# On branch master
# Changes not staged for commit:
#   (use "git add <file>..." to update what will be committed)
#   (use "git checkout -- <file>..." to discard changes in
working directory)
#     modified:   Oncemore.txt
no changes added to commit (use "git add" and/or "git commit
-a")
[pmu@t430 mydotfiles]$
```

The file shows up as modified. So, we need to add the file again like how Git instructs us to. Let's do that and see what happens.

```
[pmu@t430 mydotfiles]$ git add Oncemore.txt
[pmu@t430 mydotfiles]$ git status
# On branch master
# Changes to be committed:
#   (use "git reset HEAD <file>..." to unstage)
#     modified:   Oncemore.txt
[pmu@t430 mydotfiles]$
```

Has the checksum now changed?

```
[pmu@t430 mydotfiles]$ git ls-files --stage
100644 f10c9773eef39357a15a18183d1a4d42b349267d 0   Oncemore.
txt
100644 b70f72952f495b2aae83f2ff1a50b5ee8d001edb 0   Readme.
txt
[pmu@t430 mydotfiles]$
```

Indeed, it has. Now, Git sees this as a completely different file...or rather, a different checksum.

Now, let's run the *git commit* command with exactly the same comment we had used earlier while committing the *Oncemore.txt* file.

```
git commit -m "Now adding the Oncemore.txt file" Oncemore.txt
```

```
[pmu@t430 mydotfiles]$ git commit -m "Now adding the Oncemore.
txt file" Oncemore.txt
[master f911d56] Now adding the Oncemore.txt file
 1 file changed, 1 insertion(+)
[pmu@t430 mydotfiles]$
```

Now, we have a new *Commit Object - f911d56*. It's time for a Git push now.

Refresh your GitHub page and you'll see that the *Oncemore.txt* file has exactly the same comment that you added just two minutes before.

Well, understand that it didn't remember the comment that you ran the first time while committing *Oncemore.txt*. This is the comment that you added just now. You could have very

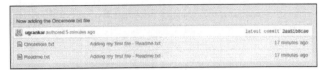

Figure 6: *Oncemore* git push

Figure 7: Modified *oncemore*

well added a different command.

Cloning from GitHub

Now that you've got your files up there on GitHub, what can you do with them? Cloning is one of them. Basically, when you clone a repo, you get a local copy of a Git repository so that you can fiddle around with it. Let's create a directory in which we will clone the repository.

Note: There is no need to run *git init* this time, because we are not creating a repo that we will be pushing up. We're just cloning an existing repository.

```
pmu@t430 mydotfiles]$ mkdir clonedir
[pmu@t430 mydotfiles]$ cd clonedir
[pmu@t430 clonedir]$ git clone  https://github.com/
ugrankar/mydotfiles.git
```

And what does it have?

```
[pmu@t430 clonedir]$ ls -la
total 0
drwxrwxr-x. 3 pmu pmu 23 Sep 22 22:44 .
drwxrwxr-x. 4 pmu pmu 68 Sep 22 22:44 ..
drwxrwxr-x. 3 pmu pmu 53 Sep 22 22:44 mydotfiles
[pmu@t430 clonedir]$ cd mydotfiles/
[pmu@t430 mydotfiles]$ ls
Oncemore.txt  Readme.txt
[pmu@t430 mydotfiles]$ ls -a
.  ..  .git  Oncemore.txt  Readme.txt
[pmu@t430 mydotfiles]$
```

There—you've got the same files that you had uploaded! END

By: Pritesh Ugrankar

The author is a Linux enthusiast. He has used CentOS 7 these past few weeks, and that has convinced him to move to it as a primary desktop. Please visit *www.priteshugrankar.wordpress. com* to check out a few interesting tweaks for CentOS 7.

Zsh: **The Ultimate Alternative to Bash**

A shell is the interface to the operating system and the services provided by it. The default shell on any operating system is the bash shell. However, there are more and better alternatives to the bash shell. Zsh is one of them.

The terms *terminal, tty, console* and *shell* are used synonymously. There is nothing wrong with that but these words mean a lot of different things. They represent pieces of hardware that were used to enter data into the computer in earlier times, as the machines back then used to be very big and data entry was done using terminals, which were also known as teletypewriters (hence, tty). Physically, they were known as consoles (from the furniture point of view). The terminal (console) in our computers these days is an application which is similar to the terminal of past days but it doesn't run on a big machine; instead, it runs on the top of the kernel in our machine. Coming to shell, it is a command interpreter that makes the use of the terminal very easy by interpreting certain characters in a specified manner—for example, tab completion in *bash*, which was absent in the older shells. In the same way, *bash* lacks some features which are covered by *zsh*.

Figure 1 shows that the shell works as an interpreter.

Different types of shell

Sh: The Bourne shell, called *sh*, is one of the original shells, developed for UNIX computers by Stephen Bourne at AT&T's Bell Labs in 1977. Its long history of use means many software developers are familiar with it. It offers features such as input and output redirection, shell scripting with string and integer variables, and condition testing and looping.

Bash: The popularity of *sh* motivated programmers to develop a shell that was compatible with it, but with several enhancements. Linux systems still offer the *sh* shell, but *bash* (the Bourne-again shell), which is based on *sh*, has become the new default standard. One attractive feature of *bash* is its ability to run *sh* shell scripts, unchanged. Shell scripts are complex sets of commands that automate programming and maintenance chores; being able to reuse these scripts saves programmers time. Conveniences not available with the original Bourne shell include command completion and a command history.

It's Good To Have A Choice!

ASSURED GIFT WITH EACH SUBSCRIPTION

1

OR

GET DISCOUNTS

2

Coffee Maker
(Worth Rs 1400)

Electronics Industry Directory 2014-15
(Worth Rs 750)

Robotics Self learning Kit
(worth Rs 2500)

EFY Round Neck T-Shift
(worth Rs 300)

Arduino Uno R3
(worth Rs 1575)

Toster Oven
(Worth Rs 2000)

Popcorn Maker
(Worth Rs 1100)

Light Following Robo
(Worth Rs 599)

OSFY Collered T-Shift
(Worth Rs 500)

8051 Pocket Programmer
(worth Rs 730)

SUBSCRIBE TO YOUR FAVOURITE MAGAZINES NOW!

Option 1: Assured Gifts with every subscription

Magazine	Duration	Issues	Cover Price (₹)	You Pay (₹)	Assured Gift
Electronics For You	1 Year	12	600	600 ☐	☐ Light Following Robo (Worth Rs 599)
	2 Years	24	1200	1200 ☐	☐ 8051 Pocket Programmer (worth Rs 730)
	3 Years	36	1800	1800 ☐	☐ Arduino Uno R3 (worth Rs 1575)
	5 Years	60	3000	3000 ☐	☐ Robotics Self learning Kit (worth Rs 2500)
Electronics Bazaar	1 Year	12	1200	1200 ☐	☐ EFY Round Neck T-Shirt (worth Rs 300)
	2 Years	24	2400	2400 ☐	☐ EYP 2014-15 (Worth Rs 750)
	3 Years	36	3600	3600 ☐	☐ Popcorn Maker (Worth Rs 1100)
	5 Years	60	6000	6000 ☐	☐ Toster Oven (Worth Rs 2000)
Open Source For You	1 Year	12	1200	1200 ☐	☐ OSFY Collered T-Shirt (Worth Rs 500)
	2 Years	24	2400	2400 ☐	☐ Popcorn Maker (Worth Rs 1100)
	3 Years	36	3600	3600 ☐	☐ Coffee Maker (Worth Rs 1400)
	5 Years	60	6000	6000 ☐	☐ Toster Oven (Worth Rs 2000)

Option 2: Upto 50% Discount Offer

Magazine	Duration	Issues	Cover Price (₹)	Discount	You Pay (₹)	You Save
Electronics For You	1 Year	12	600	20%	480 ☐	120
	2 Years	24	1200	30%	840 ☐	360
	3 Years	36	1800	40%	1080 ☐	720
	5 Years	60	3000	50%	1500 ☐	1500
Electronics Bazaar	1 Year	12	1200	20%	960 ☐	240
	2 Years	24	2400	30%	1675 ☐	725
	3 Years	36	3600	40%	2155 ☐	1445
	5 Years	60	6000	50%	2995 ☐	3005
Open Source For You	1 Year	12	1200	20%	960 ☐	240
	2 Years	24	2400	30%	1680 ☐	720
	3 Years	36	3600	40%	2160 ☐	1440
	5 Years	60	6000	50%	3000 ☐	3000

Introducing EFY's Premium Edition

Electronics For You PLUS
(With software-packed DVD)

☐ 1 Year (12 Issues) 1200 ₹ **960**
☐ 2 Yrs (24 Issues) 2400 ₹ **1800**

Free e-zine Access With Every Subscription

To Subscribe Online,
Visit: http://subscribe.efyindia.com

For Online Renewal,
Visit: http://renew.efyindia.com

- Don't Miss A Single Issue!
- Ensure Regular Supply
- FREE Replacement Policy*
- Order Now For FREE Home Delivery

* Replacement will be made if intimation of damaged / non-receipt of copies is received within 30 days of its publication
** If you are not satisfied with the magazine & services your balance amount will be returned

---

Name_____ Designation_____ Organisation_____

Mailing Address_____ City_____

Pin Code_____ State_____ Phone_____ Email_____

Subscription No. (for existing subscribers only_____. I would like to subscribe to the above (✓)marked magazine(s) starting with the next

issue. Please find enclosed a sum of Rs_____ by DD/MO/crossed cheque*bearing the No._____ dt._____ in favour of

EFY Enterprises Pvt Ltd, payable at Delhi. (*Please add Rs 50 on non-metro cheque)

Send this filled-in form or its photocopy to : **EFY Enterprises Pvt Ltd** D-87/1, Okhla Industrial Area, Phase 1, New Delhi 110 020
Ph: 011-26810601-03; Fax: 011-26817563; e-mail: **info@efy.in**

 www.efyindia.com

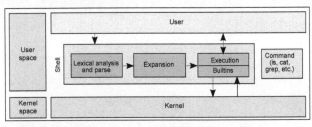

Figure 1: How the shell works

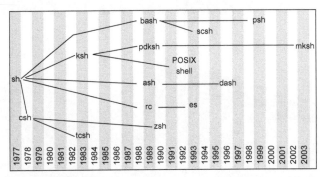

Figure 2: Different shells

Csh and Tcsh: Developers have written large parts of the Linux operating system in the C and C++ languages. Using the C syntax as a model, Bill Joy at Berkeley University developed the *C-shell (csh)* in 1978. Ken Greer, working at Carnegie-Mellon University, took *csh* concepts a step forward with a new shell called *tcsh*, which Linux systems now offer. *Tcsh* fixed problems in *csh* and added command completion, in which the shell makes educated guesses as you type, based on your system's directory structure and files. *Tcsh* does not run bash scripts, as the two have substantial differences.

Ksh: David Korn developed the *Korn shell*, or *ksh*, about the time *tcsh* was introduced. *Ksh* is compatible with *sh* and *bash*. *Ksh* improves on the Bourne shell by adding floating-point arithmetic, job control, command aliasing and command completion. AT&T held proprietary rights to *ksh* until 2000, when it became open source.

Zsh: The Z shell is the ultimate for feature-hungry users. If you can think of something that a shell ought to do, the Z shell probably does it. All that power comes at a price. For example, the *zsh* executable is nearly four times larger than the *ksh* executable and almost three times larger than the *sh* executable (Bourne shell). *Zsh* was developed by Paul Falstad.

If you want to know which shell is installed in your computer, use the following command:

```
$ ls /bin/ | grep sh
```

You can try all the shells available in your computer by just typing the name of the shell in the terminal.

Note: There are many other shells out there such as *fish* (the friendly interactive shell), *POSIX, Ash*, etc. I have given a brief on the ones that everyone knows a little about.

Why *bash*?

By default, we have the *bash* shell for users and the Bourne shell *(sh)* for the root user in Ubuntu, which has been the default since version 6.10. Fedora (Red Hat) also uses *bash* as the default shell. The major reason to switch the default shell is the efficiency of the *bash*. One day, every distro will have to shift to *zsh* as it is more efficient than *bash*.

The main features that have made *bash* the default shell in most distributions are:

- *bash* implements command aliases, and the alias and unalias built-ins

- *bash* includes a built-in help for quick reference to shell facilities
- *bash* can be customised easily by using the *~/.bashrc* file
- *bash* has process substitution
- *bash* has indirect variable expansion using *${!word}*
- *bash* implements *csh*-like history expansion

You can get a list of all the major differences from the following link:

http://www.gnu.org/software/bash/manual/html_node/Major-Differences-From-The-Bourne-Shell.html

Shell scripting

These are the rules that must not be forgotten while writing a script:

- The first line should be *#!/bin/sh*
- You must change the permissions of the file to execute it —*chmod a+x filename*
- Always use comments to explain the code; if the first character is '#', then the line is treated as a comment.
- Use the *echo* command to explain what is happening in the background when the shell is running.
- The extension of the file need not be *.sh*
  Here's my first shell code:

```
#! /bin/sh
# my first script

echo "Hello World"
```

The first line says that this is a code that needs to be executed using the Bourne shell. The second line is a comment as it starts with *#. Echo* just prints whatever exists within the " ".

```
#! /bin/sh
# greeting script

echo "Hi    $USER"
echo "Have a nice day !!!!!!!!!"
```

Echo substitutes the *$USER* with the username logged in and prints the greetings.

```
#! /bin/sh
# greeting with reading name

echo "Hi $USER"
echo "Please enter your real name"
read a;
echo "Thank you for entering your name"
echo "Have a nice day $a !!!!"

exit 0
```

The *read* takes the input and saves it in the variable *a*. And the *echo* command prints the name by substituting it in the *$a*. *Exit* just exits from the program.

In *bash*, you can use syntax that is similar to C (programming language). Here is a script which prints all the files that are executable in the given directory.

> **Note:** It also returns the directories (folders) because the folders also have the executable permission.

```
#!/bin/bash
# find all executables
count=0
# Test arguments
if [ $# -ne 1 ] ; then
  echo "Usage is $0 <dir>"
  exit 1
fi
# Ensure argument is a directory
if [ ! -d "$1" ] ; then
  echo "$1 is not a directory."
  exit 1
fi
# Iterate the directory, emit executable files
for filename in "$1"/*
do
  if [ -x "$filename" ] ; then
    echo $filename
    count=$((count+1))
  fi
done
echo
echo "$count executable files found."
exit 0
```

In this script, the thing that is newly added is the *if* statement. As you can see, the syntax is a bit different and you should also use *then* after the *if*. Besides, the brackets used for *if* are a bit different.

How to install *zsh*

Installing *zsh* is very easy. It can be done from your package manager based on your distribution, using the following command, which you can also use to update the *zsh* if you had

```
zsh-newuser-install.
You are seeing this message because you have no zsh startup files
(the files .zshenv, .zprofile, .zshrc, .zlogin in the directory
~). This function can help you with a few settings that should
make your use of the shell easier.

You can:

(q)  Quit and do nothing.  The function will be run again next time.

(0)  Exit, creating the file ~/.zshrc containing just a comment.
     That will prevent this function being run again.

(1)  Continue to the main menu.

(2)  Populate your ~/.zshrc with the configuration recommended
     by the system administrator and exit (you will need to edit
     the file by hand, if so desired).

--- Type one of the keys in parentheses ---
```

Figure 3: zsh-newuser-tall

already installed it.

For Ubuntu- or Debian-based distros, type:

```
sudo apt-get install zsh
```

For Red Hat-based distros, type:

```
sudo yum install zsh
```

For SUSE-based distros, type:

```
sudo zypper install zsh
```

For Arch Linux or Manjaro, type:

```
sudo pacman -S zsh
```

You can try using the *zsh* shell by just typing *zsh* in a terminal. If you are using *zsh* for the first time, you will get four options with a heading *zsh-newuser-install*.

Now type '0' and it goes to a basic *zsh* which looks like it lacks features in comparison to *bash*. But don't uninstall *zsh* and shift back to the old *bash* as there is more to be installed. You can modify *zsh* to fit your needs by modifying the *.zshrc* file, using the following command:

```
vi ~/.zshrc
```

> **Note:** You can use whichever editor you want instead of Vim to edit the *.zshrc* file, though I prefer Vim. We can skip this and use a readymade *zsh* configuration such as *oh-my-zsh*.

Installing *oh-my-zsh*

oh-my-zsh is an open source, community-driven framework for managing your *zsh* configuration. It comes with lots of helpful functions, helpers, plugins, themes, and a few things that make *zsh* more user friendly. You can find more about it from its website *http://ohmyz.sh/* and you can

Figure 4: *zsh* logo

Figure 5: Installing *zsh* using *wget*

contribute to it at *https://github.com/robbyrussell/oh-my-zsh*. It can be installed in two ways, either by using *Curl* or *wget*. oh-my-zsh uses Git, so you need to first install some packages in order to be able to install *oh-my-zsh*. Here's a list of them:

```
sudo apt-get install git-core curl
```

If you are using *Curl*, type:

```
curl -Lhttp ://install.ohmyz.sh | sh
```

If you are using *wget*, type:

```
wget --no-check-certificate http://install.ohmyz.sh -O - | sh
```

Figure 5 shows how the installation looks on a Ubuntu 14.04 system.

If we use the above two commands, *oh-my-zsh* installs itself automatically. You can install it using *git* in the following manner:

```
p ~/git clone git://github.com/robbyrussell/oh-my-zsh.git
~/.oh-my-zsh
cp ~/.zshrc ~/.zshrc.old
cp oh-my-zsh .o.oh-my-zsh/templates/zshrc.zsh-template
~/.zshrc
```

Setting *zsh* as the default shell

By default, *bash* is set as the shell in most modern distributions. You can change the default shell by using the *chsh* command:

```
chsh -s /bin/zsh username
```

Here, *username* is the one with which you are logged in. You can do the same with the root user but add *sudo* in front of it, as changing the shell for the root requires more privileges.

> **Note:** By default, *oh-my-zsh* is installed only for the user.

Themes

By default, *oh-my-zsh* is set to its own theme, but you can set it to whatever you want to by changing line 10 *of ~/.zshrc* to *random* or the name of the *zsh-theme* available on *~/.oh-my-zsh/themes/*. You can also choose your favourite themes by running the following commands at a terminal. There are a lot of themes available, and each has a different purpose -- some show the time, others show the battery level, etc.

```
cd ~/.oh-my-zsh/tools/
./theme_chooser.sh
```

After typing the above command, you will be shown a cool heading as the *zsh theme chooser,* which displays the preview of all the themes available in the folder *~/.oh-my-zsh/themes/* and asks whether to add the given template to your *favourites* list. There are also many tools available in the tools directory of *.oh-my-zsh.*

Updating *oh-my-zsh*

Updating *oh-my-zsh* is very easy. It can be done by typing *upgrade_oh_my_zsh* on the command line.

Why is zsh better than bash?

Here are a few reasons.

It's similar to bash: The foremost plus point of *zsh* is that it is backward-compatible with *bash*. Every valid command in *bash* becomes a valid command of *zsh* (except for a very few exceptions). Even if the *zsh* was more powerful than *bash,* it would have not been used by any one if it had some new and weird syntax. So if you know how to use a normal command line *(bash),* then you know the most powerful shell *(zsh)* syntax.

Spelling mistakes: It corrects almost all the spelling mistakes when you're using the command line. For example, in bash, if you type *cd /deskt* and press the tab, it doesn't give us anything, but in *zsh*, it changes itself to *cd /Desktop.*

Intelligent tab completion: The tab completion doesn't just complete the last command but also checks for the whole line. For example, if you type *cd /u/lo/b* and hit a tab, it changes to *cd /usr/local/bin/.* Similarly, when you type *cd /u/l*

Figure 6: Upgrading *oh-my-zsh*

it expands till *cd /usr/l*, before asking you if you mean *lib* or *local*, as there is a chance of either being the right choice.

Command history: This is one of the most important features. In *bash*, if we type some command and press the up arrow a number of times, we get the whole history. But in *zsh*, if we type a command and use the arrow button, we only get the commands that have the specific command in it. As an example, the order in which we typed the commands is shown below:

```
cat /etc/passwd
cd ~
cd /root
cat
```

In *bash*, if we type 'cat' and then the arrow key, we get *cd /root* but in *zsh*, we go directly to the cat */etc/passwd* as *zsh* gives the history of the specific command.

Sharing history across sessions: If you are running two different *zsh* sessions, whatever command we typed last can be shared with any of the other terminals with *zsh*. This can't be done in *bash*.

Extended globbing: Globbing means the use of '*' to match all the items—in *zsh*, we can use '**' to match even the directory that is located very deep.

Easy scripting: With *zsh*, we can do shell scripting very easily because it has a more tolerable syntax. (Even though I don't recommend using it as it is not installed in every machine by default. But it can be used locally for daily work if one is too lazy to type a particular instruction every day).

Aliases: By default, *zsh* has many aliases, which are mainly typing errors.

Many other features: *Zsh* supports many other features such as *git* completion, the built-in *less* command, etc. *zsh*, along with the configuration of *oh-my-zsh*, turns into a powerful tool and makes the command line interface more friendly.

> **Note:** Some themes in *oh-my-zsh* may not work in a proper manner. So you can report the problems at *https://github.com/robbyrussell/oh-my-zsh/issues*

Uninstalling *zsh/oh-my-zsh*

Zsh is a very good shell that you may not be interested in uninstalling. In case you don't like the *oh-my-zsh* configuration, you can uninstall it using the simple command shown below:

```
uninstall_oh_my_zsh
```

This removes the *oh-my-zsh* and restores the *.zshrc* which was configured before installing *oh-my-zsh*. If you don't want *zsh* at all, then you can run the following command:

```
sudo apt-get remove zsh
sudo apt-get remove --purge zsh
```

> **Note:** If even after using the above commands the configuration files in *.zshrc* do not get removed, you need to remove them manually by using *rm -rf ~/.zshrc*, or by using *Ctrl+H* (to show the hidden files in Nautilus) and pressing *Shift + Delete* (to delete them permanently without saving them to *Trash*)

References

[1] *http://www.wikipedia.org/*
[2] *http://www.ibm.com/developerworks/linux/library/l-linux-shells/*
[3] *http://ohmyz.sh/*

By: Tummala Dhanvi

The author is a security engineer who specialises in reverse engineering. He is also a member of team biOs. He can be contacted at *dhanvicse@gmail.com*

A Few Good Things about the Tab Page Feature in Vim

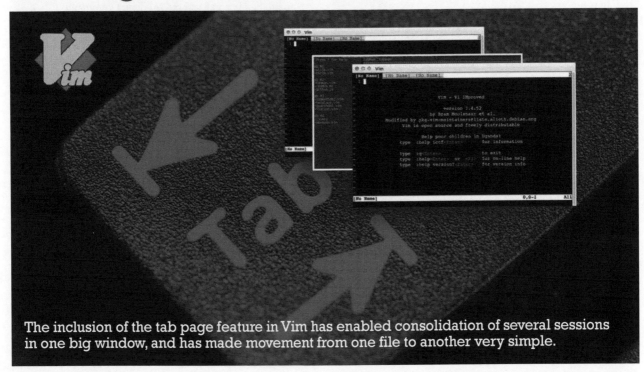

The inclusion of the tab page feature in Vim has enabled consolidation of several sessions in one big window, and has made movement from one file to another very simple.

Almost every graphical text editor provides a tab page feature. At first sight, it appears that Vim may have missed out on this hefty feature, but that's not true. Vim has great support for tab pages. It even allows the opening of multiple files under the same tab page via a window-splitting feature. The tab page feature was introduced in Vim in version 7.0 (released in May 2006). It is considered one of the best features of Vim. This column explores the tab page feature of the Vim editor. It is assumed that readers have some basic understanding of Vim.

Before delving deep into tab page features, let us understand how tabs are different from buffers and windows. Files store data on the disk in a persistent manner, whereas buffers reside in the memory. A buffer is an in-memory representation of a file. When we open any file in Vim, it is loaded into the buffer, and even when we perform any changes, we are actually modifying the buffer. For instance, the command below loads contents of the two files in separate buffers.

```
[bash]$ vim file1.txt file2.txt
```

We can easily switch to the next buffer by executing the *:bnext* command.

A window is a view-port into a buffer. Vim allows the viewing of multiple buffers side by side by dividing the workspace into multiple windows. Each window can open the same or a different buffer. Windows can be split either horizontally or vertically. A tab page is just a collection of one or more windows placed side by side. We can also open multiple windows inside each tab page. Shortly, we will look at an example of the same.

Working with tab pages

Now that we have learned theoretical fundamentals of tab pages, it's time to do something practical. We can instruct Vim to open tab pages in multiple ways. One of the easiest is to open tab pages at start-up. The syntax of Vim's command-line argument to open multiple tab pages is given below.

```
vim -p[N]
```

In the above syntax, 'N' implies the number of tab pages and square bracket implies it's an optional parameter. To open three tab pages at start-up, use the command shown below.

```
[bash]$ vim -p3
```

Please note that *-p3* is a single word. This command opens three empty tab pages as shown in Figure 1.

Alternatively, we can also provide files to open them in

separate tab pages. For instance, the command below instructs Vim to open each file in a new tab page.

```
[bash]$ vim  p file1.txt file2.txt
```

If the number of tab pages is greater than the number of files provided at the command line, then the remaining tab pages open empty buffers. For instance, the command below opens a total of four tab pages, where the first two show *file1.txt* and *file2.txt*, respectively, while the remaining two show empty buffers.

```
[bash] vim -p4 file1.txt file2.txt
```

What if we want to open a tab page in the middle of our work? Don't worry about it. There is no need to close the current Vim session. Vim developers have already thought about this. There are two more commands, using which we can open tab pages in a running instance of Vim. We can use either of the following three commands— *:tabnew, :tabedit* or *:tabe*. The syntax for each command is given below:

```
:[N]tabnew [filename]
:[N]tabe [filename]
:[N]tabedit [filename]
```

If you omit the file name with the above commands then Vim opens empty tab pages; otherwise, it loads the file into a new tab page. If 'N' is omitted, the new tab page appears after the current one; otherwise, Vim opens a new tab page after the Nth tab page.

Tab pages are really awesome. But the question is: how many tab pages can we open? By default, we can open up to 10 tab pages, but this behaviour can be controlled by setting the *tabpagemax* option. For instance, to set an upper cap of 20 tab pages, add the following line into *~/.vimrc:*

```
set tabpagemax=20
```

If the number of tabs allowed by *tabpagemax* is exceeded, Vim will simply open the maximum number of tabs, and the other files will be opened but not displayed. You can edit the remaining files by using the *:next* or *:last* commands to move to the files that are not displayed in the tab pages. Please note that this setting is applicable only for the *'-p'* option; you can open as many tab pages as you like from a running instance of Vim.

In addition to this, Vim also provides the *tabfind* or *tabf* command, which finds the file in the current path and opens it in a new tab page. It uses Vim's *path* option to determine which directories should be searched when opening the specified file. To determine the value of the current path, just execute the *:set path* command. On my system, its value is as follows:

```
path=.,/usr/include,,
```

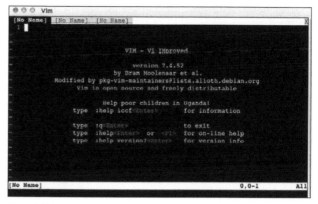

Figure 1: Tab pages

The above *path* instructs Vim to look in the directory containing the current file *(period(.))*, then the */usr/include* directory and, finally, the current directory (the empty text between two commas). To append an additional search path, execute the following command:

```
:set path += /etc
```

The steps below demonstrate how to use the *tabfind* command to find and open files in a new tab page:

```
[bash]$ cd /tmp/test      # Deliberately switch to the empty
                            directory.

[bash]$ ls                # Verify it is empty.

[bash]$ vim               # Open instance of vim and execute
                            the command below from vim
:tabfind malloc.h
```

Though the */tmp/test* directory doesn't contain the *malloc.h* file, Vim opens it by searching for it in the */usr/include* path. You can also use regular expressions with *tabfind*. Just as in the *:tabedit* command, when 'N' is omitted with the *:tabfind* command, a new tab page appears after the current one; otherwise, Vim opens a new tab page after the Nth tab page.

So far, we have seen several ways to open tab pages. Now, let us quickly go through the steps to close the tab pages. To close tab pages, we can use any of the following commands according to our requirements:

```
:tabclose
:tabclose [N]
:tabonly
```

As the name suggests, the *:tabclose* command closes the current tab page. But this command may fail, if the current tab page is the last tab page or the in-memory buffer is modified but not yet written to the disk.

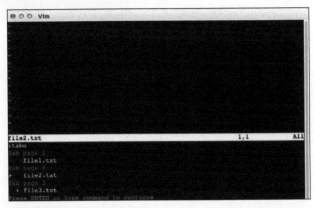

Figure 2: Tabs

The *:tabclose [N]* command closes the Nth tab page. This command can fail in the same way as the *:tabclose* command. Please note that the tab page counting begins from '1'. For instance, to close the third tab page, use the syntax below:

```
:tabclose 3
```

The *:tabonly* command closes all other tab pages and shows the current tab page only. This command execution can fail if the in-memory buffer of any tab page is modified but not yet written to the disk. In addition to this, to close the current tab, we can use Vim's regular commands as well—for instance, *:wq, :q!, :x, ZZ* and so on.

Navigating tab pages

Vim provides several ways to get information about tab pages. For instance, the *:tabs* command provides a summary of all open tabs. It shows a > symbol for the current window and shows a + symbol for modified buffers. Figure 2 illustrates this.

By default, tab page labels are shown at the top of the Vim window only when tab pages are open. To display tab page labels all the time, use the following command:

```
:set showtabline=2
```

Similarly, to hide the tab page labels, use *0* instead of *2* in the above command.

We can use any of the commands below to navigate tab pages:

```
:tabn
:tabn [N]
:tabnext
:tabnext [N]
:tabN
:tabN [N]
:tabNext
:tabNext [N]
:tabp
:tabp [N]
```

```
:tabprevious
:tabprevious [N]
```

As the name suggests, the *:tabn* command jumps to the next tab page. Tab page navigation wraps around from the last to the first one. For instance, if there are five tab pages open and currently we are at the fifth tab page, then execution of the *:tabn* command causes it to go to the first tab page. Similarly, *:tabn [N]* jumps to the Nth tab page. *:tabnext* and *:tabnext [N]* work exactly like the *:tabn* and *:tabn [N]* commands, respectively.

The *:tabN* command jumps to the previous tab page. Tab page navigation wraps around from the first one to the last one. For instance, if there are five tab pages open and currently we are at the first tab page, then execution of the *:tabN* command causes it to go to the fifth tab page. Similarly, *:tabN [N]* goes N tab pages back. *:tabNext* and *:tabNext [N]* work exactly similar to the *:tabN* and *:tabN [N]* commands, respectively.

The *:tabp* and *:tabprevious* commands work exactly the same way as the *:tabN* command. The *:tabprevious [N]* and *:tabp [N]* commands work the same way as the *:tabN [N]* command.

In addition to this, we can directly jump to the first or last tab page by using the following commands.

The *:tabfirst* or *:tabrewind* command jumps to the first tab page. Similarly, the *:tablast* command jumps to the last tab page. Vim also allows tab page navigation in command and insert mode. For instance, in command mode, we can use the following commands.

gt : Jumps to the next tab page. Tab page navigation wraps around from the last to the first one.

gT : Jumps to the previous tab page. Tab page navigation wraps around from the first one to the last one.

[N]gt : Jumps to the 'N'th tab page in forward direction. Tab page navigation wraps around from the last to the first one.

[N]gT : Jumps to the 'N'th tab page in backward direction. Tab page navigation wraps around from the first one to the last one.

In addition to the above commands, we can use the following tab page navigation commands either in command or insert mode.

Ctrl + PageDown : Jumps to the next tab page. Tab page navigation wraps around from the last to the first one.

Ctrl + PageUp: Jumps to the previous tab page. Tab page navigation wraps around from the first one to the last one.

[N]Ctrl + PageDown: Jumps to the 'N'th tab page in forward direction. Tab page navigation wraps around from the last to the first one.

[N]Ctrl + PageUp: Jumps to the 'N'th tab page in backward direction. Tab page navigation wraps around from the first one to the last one.

Miscellaneous commands

We have seen that we can open and navigate tab pages in any order. Wouldn't it be great if we could rearrange the order of the tab pages according to our choice? This can certainly be done by using the following set of commands:

```
:tabmove
:tabmove 0
:tabmove [N]
:tabm
:tabm 0
:tabm [N]
```

The *:tabmov* command moves the current tab page to the last position. To move the current tab page to the first position, execute the following command:

```
:tabmove 0
```

Similarly, the *:tabmove [N]* command moves the current tab page to the N + 1th position. Please note that the *:tabmove* command counts tab pages from zero. Hence, *:tabmove 4* moves the current tab page to the fifth position. *:tabm* is just the abbreviated form of the *:tabmove* command.

The *:tabdo* or *:tabd* commands are extremely useful when we want to execute certain commands in each tab page. Here is the syntax of the command:

```
:tabdo <command>
:tabd <command>
```

Here, the angular bracket implies the command is mandatory. Listed below is the workflow of the *:tabdo* command.
Step 1: Go to the first tab page.
Step 2: Execute the specified command in the current tab page.
Step 3: If it is a last tab page then stop the execution of the command.
Step 4: Otherwise jump to the next tab page and go to Step 2.

Let us suppose that we have opened multiple tab pages and want to replace the word 'Tom' with 'Jerry' on each tab page; then the following command will do the needful:

```
:tabdo %s/\<Tom\>/Jerry
```

Please note that one of the limitations of this command is that it can only execute the same command in each tab page.

Vim already supports the command that works nicely with split windows. Vim provides the *:tab* command line modifier to use a new tab page instead of a new window for commands that would normally split a window. For instance, the *:tab ball* command shows each buffer in a separate tab page. The simple example given below illustrates the same.

```
[bash]$ vim file1.txt file2.txt file3.txt
```

In the above command, Vim opens three files in separate buffers but only shows a single buffer/ window at a time. We can use the *:bnext* command to switch to the next buffer. Now, to open these buffers into separate tab pages, execute the *:tab ball* command from the current Vim session.

Additionally, we can view Vim's help contents in a new tab page. By default, the *:help* command splits the window horizontally and displays help contents in the split window. To view help contents in a separate tab page, execute the following command from the Vim session, as shown below:

```
:tab help
```

Similarly, the *:tab split [filename]* command opens a file in a new tab page rather than splitting he window. If the *filename* is omitted with this command, it copies the current window to a new tab page. Otherwise, it opens the specified file in a new tab page. For instance, the command below opens the *file1.txt* file in a new tab page.

```
[bash]$ vim file1.txt # Now execute the command below from Vim
:tab split
```

Wouldn't it be great if we could use both tab pages and split window features together? Vim provides that flexibility. Let us suppose you have opened several files in a split window and you want to move a certain file to a new tab page. Just press *Ctrl+W T*. Similarly, to close the current tab page, use the *Ctrl+W c* key combination.

We can also use the *goto* file feature with the tab pages. By using this, we can put the cursor on the file name and open the file into a new tab page by pressing the *Ctrl+W gf* key combination. The example below illustrates this feature:

```
[bash]$ echo "This is file#1" > file1.txt

[bash]$ echo "file1.txt" > file2.txt

[bash]$ vim file2.txt # Now execute the command below from Vim
Ctrl+W gf or
Ctrl+W gF
```

This will open *file1.txt* in a new tab page. Please note that you must set the appropriate 'path' option to use this feature.

Myriad tasks can be done with Vim. Only a few keystrokes are required to solve complex tasks. These simple yet powerful features really make Vim more interesting. To gain insights into tab pages, go through Vim's help documentation. You can access the document by executing the *:help tab-page-intro* command from the Vim session. END

By: Narendra Kangralkar

The author is a FOSS enthusiast and loves exploring anything related to open source. He can be reached at narendrakangralkar@gmail.com

Will Bitcoin Rule the Free World?

Bitcoin is digital currency that uses peer-to-peer technology to enable instant payments to anyone. It uses open source software called Bitcoin Core to enable the use of the currency.

Every once in a while, a new idea is born—one that has the potential to question the very foundations of everything we know about the world as it is today. The ideas I am talking about are those that have changed and will change the world for the better. Take email, for example —at its inception, people thought it was for the geeks and wouldn't catch on. I would have agreed in the early days, but look at how the world has become so dependent on it over the last few decades. This is an ongoing phenomenon—what is old will either perish or evolve. The only constant, if any, is change.

On a cold winter morning of January 2009, Satoshi Nakamoto set out to change the way we transact business and unleashed the world's first cryptocurrency, bitcoin.

A cryptocurrency is a form of digital currency that uses cryptography (the science of hiding messages in codes that appear to be a random string of characters) as a means of generating new units and securing transactions. Its heavy dependence on cryptography is how it derived its name.

Though Bitcoin is by far the most popular cryptocurrency, a few others like Litecoin and Ripple are also gaining momentum.

The history of Bitcoin

In 2008, Satoshi Nakamoto, founder of Bitcoin, published a paper titled Bitcoin: A Peer-to-Peer Electronic Cash System (*http://goo.gl/MqyCW7*), which explained in detail how a peer-to-peer (P2P) currency would work. In January 2009, he officially launched the Bitcoin network. Complementing that, he also launched the Bitcoin Core software (*http://goo.gl/gUbUq*), which would help people mine (a term explained later) and trade (please refer to *An Introduction to Bitcoin: The Open Source Cryptographic Currency*, published in the November 2013 edition of *Open Source For You)* in bitcoins. The Bitcoin Project was released under the MIT licence, which essentially meant that it's free and open source. The new currency rapidly gained momentum and became the talk of the town. It proved to be a nightmare for banks and governments worldwide but it became the darling of the online underworld (for reasons that I will go into later).

After launching Bitcoin, Satoshi Nakamoto gradually disappeared from the online world leaving his creation in the hands of the community, which was by then swearing by it. Surprisingly, in this well-connected and spied-upon world, Nakamoto still remains a mysterious figure. While many have speculated about who he really is, no one has arrived at any conclusive proof about his identity. Given the complexity and sophistication of the Bitcoin system, many researchers believe that it can't be the work of a single person. They believe that some kind of group or consortium of technology companies is behind this cryptocurrency. Considering that Bitcoin mining is processing power-intensive, these companies would surely stand to benefit from selling the concept to the Bitcoin community.

What is a bitcoin?

Given its name and logo, people mistakenly assume that it is a physical coin with electromagnetic capabilities, which is contrary to the very notion of a cryptocurrency. The essence of a cryptocurrency is that it is not required to and cannot exist in a physical form.

The following analogy will help you understand the concept of Bitcoin better. Let's say you have 10,000 units of a currency in a bank account and you can conduct online transactions with this account. At any given moment,

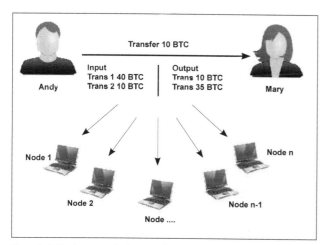

Figure 1: A bitcoin transaction between Andy and Mary

the amount of currency available to you for conducting transactions is the cumulative sum of all the transactions you've performed till date via that account. Now, as long as you don't withdraw the amount physically, it's just a number stored in the bank's database. When you perform an online transaction, using this account, it is recorded in your account —the relevant number is either deducted from your account or credited to it, depending on the nature of your transaction. Again, as long as you don't withdraw the balance amount physically, it exists in a virtual state in the bank's database. This is what bitcoin is, except that with bitcoins, you are your own bank; your bitcoin wallet is your bank account and you can't withdraw it physically. You can exchange it in return for some other currency but you can't have bitcoins in physical form because they only exist in digital (or virtual) form.

"Thou shalt remain in states of 0s and 1s forever…"

"Hey! Hold on…I have to first deposit 10,000 units of hard cash with the bank before they can become virtual and here you're saying that bitcoin only exists in virtual from. How does this work? Where are all these bitcoins coming from?"

Bitcoins originate via a process called bitcoin mining. Before I delve more into it, let's understand how the Bitcoin network works and how a transaction takes place. As I mentioned earlier, Bitcoin is a peer-to-peer network, which means that there's no single entity controlling it. It is a decentralised network and each system in this network acts as a node.

Let's assume that Andy and Mary are conducting a transaction in bitcoin (BTC), in which Andy wants to transfer 10 BTC to Mary in return for a service and he currently has a total of 50 BTC in his bitcoin wallet. Figure 1 depicts how the transaction between them would look.

There are two parts to this transaction—the input and output. The input part contains a reference to the previous transactions, which would account for the amount of BTC currently in Andy's wallet. The output part will contain the information of how many bitcoins Andy wants to transfer (10 BTC in this case) and how much change he wants back

(35 BTC in this case). The difference between the amount he wants to transfer and the change he wants back, if any, is the transaction fee (5 BTC in this case). The transaction fee is the incentive for bitcoin miners to include that transaction in a transaction block (explained later). Andy will then sign this transaction with his digital signature and publish it to the Bitcoin network. All nodes in the Bitcoin network will receive this transaction. They may or may not act upon it, depending on their role in the network.

A bitcoin miner is a node in the Bitcoin network, running bitcoin mining software. A bitcoin mining node collects Andy's transaction, along with many others, and collates them into what is called a transaction block. If this block is accepted by the network, it will then be appended to the universal transaction block chain. Think of the transaction block chain as a universal ledger which has all the transactions recorded in it, since the beginning of the Bitcoin system. Once the miners' transaction blocks are accepted, they are rewarded with a certain number of bitcoins (in addition to the transaction fee) that accrues from all the transactions included in that block. This reward part is how new bitcoins are created in the Bitcoin network.

On the face of it, the bitcoin mining process might seem to be a very simplistic process, but it actually involves its share of complexity. The Bitcoin network doesn't simply accept a transaction block—a miner has to prove the effort he has put in while working on that transaction block. This is called 'proof of work'.

Proof of work is a cryptographic puzzle, which the Bitcoin network requires the miner to solve before the transaction block is accepted within the transaction block chain. The creation of a transaction block is fairly simple and doesn't require much effort; solving this puzzle is what makes mining a processing power-intensive task. The difficulty level of the puzzle is decided by the Bitcoin network, which is designed to adjust it, depending on how fast transaction blocks are being generated. If it senses that blocks are being generated too fast, the network increases the difficulty level and vice versa. The miner who solves the proof of work puzzle first, publishes the solution on the network. The Bitcoin network then verifies the solution sent by the miner, and if correct, the transaction block is appended to the transaction block chain. Though generating the solution is processing power-intensive, verifying it hardly takes any time.

While mining is one way in which bitcoins circulate, there are three much simpler ways:

- Exchanging bitcoins in return for some other currency, either from a designated exchange or from a person willing to make such an exchange. It's 100 per cent legal, as of date, though the Reserve Bank of India advises against it (*http://goo.gl/fbh3wO*).
- Accepting bitcoins for a service or product.
- Asking a friend for some (this might be bit tricky, given the current value of the bitcoin).

What about securing this 'currency'?

"Hmm…so how secure is it? With other currencies, I've got banks and their robust systems protecting my money, but this sounds like it's all on me."

Well, that's both true and false. With bitcoins, you'll need to be a bit more careful but such is the case with banks too. If you're casual in handling your bank account numbers and passwords, there is a fairly high risk of you losing your money even from your supposedly 'safe' bank account.

Besides, the foundation of Bitcoin is laid using one of the principle elements of information security, which is cryptography. Unless somebody invents a supercomputer that can break the sophisticated algorithms at play in the Bitcoin network (some agencies are trying hard but even they haven't achieved any significant progress on this front yet), there's only a very small likelihood of the network getting breached.

This brings us to the second most common concern when dealing with currency—fraud. There have been very few successful attempts to fraud the Bitcoin network but even those didn't last long. Security researchers have tried to break in but they couldn't (http://goo.gl/fSlsMZ).

Still, let's assume that somebody does give it a shot. Since the sanctity of the Bitcoin network is dependent on the transaction block chain, the most common way to fraud the system would be to introduce malicious transactions in the chain. Carrying forward the earlier-mentioned example, let's assume that Andy has malicious intentions and he wants to cheat Mary. Right after his transaction with her, he creates another transaction in which he transfers the 10 BTC back to himself.

On an average, every 10 minutes a transaction block is added to the transaction block chain and once this is added, the miners stop working with the previous block and start on the one that's just added. At any given moment, there are thousands of miners putting together their processing power simultaneously to honestly mine bitcoins.

If Andy wants to introduce the malicious transaction in the chain, he has to create a new transaction block with that transaction in it, and challenge not only the transaction block in which his first transaction was but also all the ones added after that. The challenge for Andy is to solve the 'proof of work' puzzle for the block that has the genuine transaction and for each block in the chain, after that particular one. This boils down to the processing power available with him, competing with the processing power available with thousands of honest bitcoin miners. Unless Andy has resources to obtain that kind of processing power and a much bigger incentive than his investment, he's not going to make it.

The fraud that Andy was trying to commit in the above example is called double-spending, i.e., spending exactly the same money twice. In the banking system, banks and payment gateways usually monitor systems for double-spending. In the Bitcoin network, the network itself takes care of it, as long as the processing power of honest miners is more than that of a fraudster.

The Bitcoin network has another security enhancement that beats the current banking system, and that is anonymity. Similar to the banking system, in the Bitcoin network too your wallet is represented by a string of seemingly random characters but that's all they have in common on this front. The Bitcoin network doesn't need to know who you are, nor your address, age and other details—all of which are required by the banking system.

The pros and cons

"I've heard you out. But I am still sceptical…"

Like every other thing out there, bitcoins also ship with a list of pros and cons.

The pros:

- The Bitcoin network is decentralised, which means no single authority, bank or government can control or regulate it. Therefore, it is inflation-proof.
- There's no third party involved while transacting in bitcoins. It's all person-to-person.
- Even though the transactions are public, it provides complete anonymity. People can know how much balance a particular account has but they can't find out who owns that account.
- There are no bank fees, credit card charges, service charges, etc. A bitcoin can be transferred from one account to another at the click of a key, irrespective of the country, state or city.
- The transactions done in bitcoins are irreversible and thereby prevent merchants from fraud purchases.
- Anyone with an Internet connection can deal in bitcoins.

The cons:

- The network is highly volatile. Unless you're a miner, you'll have to buy bitcoins with alternate currency. The exchange rate of a bitcoin is purely governed by demand and supply. When it started out, the exchange rate was US$ .0008 per BTC and achieved a maximum rate of $1100 per BTC in November 2013 (http://goo.gl/pqQ7L).
- There is a potential for the bitcoin to lose value if a better cryptocurrency crops up.
- It's irrecoverable. Unfortunately, if you lose access to your bitcoin wallet, there's no way to get it back. You'll have to write it off.
- Governments are staying away from it.

What you might be wondering…

- ***Can the governments completely ban Bitcoin?***
  As mentioned earlier, bitcoins are not issued by any government, so they literally have no say in how it's circulated. This also means that they cannot completely

ban bitcoins. However, they can make dealing in it illegal. But even then, there's no way for the state to track who's dealing in bitcoins because of the anonymity it provides. Besides, even if some countries ban it, not all governments will share the same viewpoint.

- *Why are governments and banks sceptical of Bitcoin?*
Why does anybody fear anything? Either they don't understand it or are threatened by it. I am sure we can cross off the former reason. Governments and banks are feeling threatened because they have genuine reason to be. Bitcoin is questioning the way currency and banks work and the latter don't know how it's going to turn out. They can speculate for sure, but nothing is certain. In simple words, governments and banks are afraid to lose control.

- *People believe it to be a Ponzi scheme. Are they right?*
The main principle at work in any Ponzi scheme is that there's a single entity behind it. This entity has malicious intentions and at an opportune moment, runs away with the money. With Bitcoin, there's no single entity controlling it. All the work is done by nodes and miners. There might have been a possibility of a backdoor in the software code, but it's open source! Any such bug, flaw or backdoor would be visible to the community and will be fixed before any harm can be caused.

- *Is it possible to take down the Bitcoin network?*
Yes, if the community loses faith in it, it may decide not to be a part of the network. However, it'll be a very difficult task for any government or national agency to take down the network because it has spread across the world. It's very similar to the BitTorrent network. Even if they do take it down, the source code is available to anyone. A similar network can be created by anyone, anywhere in the world.

- *Is it safe to invest in bitcoin?*
Personally, I would advise against it. However, if you

Did you know?

- Only a limited number of bitcoins can be mined in total. The cap is set at 21 million and this quota is expected to be mined by 2140.
- The reward which is assigned to a miner upon successful mining is set to decrease by half every time a 210,000th transaction block is generated. It takes approximately four years to generate 210,000 transaction blocks. The reward started with 50 BTC and is currently set at 25 BTC.
- Bitcoin (with a capital B) is used to denote the Bitcoin network and bitcoin (with a small b) is used to denote the currency.
- The minimum denomination in which bitcoins can be dealt is .00000001. This is called a Satoshi.
- The German Ministry of Finance has officially recognised bitcoin as a valid currency.
- On October 29, 2013, the world's first Bitcoin ATM went online in Vancouver, Canada. It was installed by a company named Bitcoiniacs.
- A Malta-based company named Exante Ltd has created the world's first bitcoin-based hedge fund.

wish to experiment, either wait till the exchange rate drops or ask a friend.

A more exhaustive list of frequently asked questions about Bitcoin is available at *http://goo.gl/x1Tm7m*.

Satoshi Nakamoto has started a revolution in the form of Bitcoin which, if successful, holds the potential to replace the concept of currencies as we know it. More and more people are seeing value in dealing in bitcoins. Today, you can buy a beer, pizza, groceries, etc, by paying in bitcoins. Going by the current trend, it would seem that Bitcoin is here to stay. END

By: Uday Mittal

The author can be contacted at *mailme@udaymittal.com*.

Learn How to Visualise Graph Theory

The focus now shifts from Maxima's computation features to its capabilities in visualising graphs. In this article, the author discusses the drawing of graphs in Maxima.

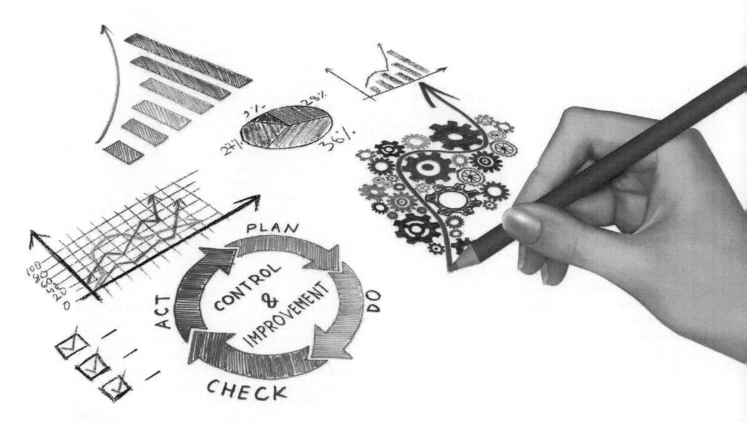

This 23rd article on the mathematical journey through open source introduces graph theory with visuals, using the graphs package of Maxima.

Graphs here refer to the structures formed using some points (or vertices) and some lines (or edges) connecting them. A simple example would be a graph with two vertices, say '0' and '1', and an edge between '0' and '1'. If all the edges of a graph have a sense of direction from one vertex to another, typically represented by an arrow at their end(s), we call that a directed graph with directed edges. In such a case, we consider the edges as not between two vertices but from one vertex to another. Directed edges are also referred to as arcs. In the above example, we could have two directed arcs, one from '0' to '1', and another from '1' to '0'. Figures 1 and 2 show an undirected and a directed graph, respectively.

Graph creation and visualisation

Now, how did we get those figures? We got them by using the graphs package of Maxima, which is loaded by invoking *load(graphs)* at the Maxima prompt. In the package, vertices are represented by whole numbers 0, 1, ... and

an edge is represented as a list of its two vertices. Using these notations, we can create graphs using the *create_graph(<vertex_list>, <edge_list>[, directed])* function. And then *draw_graph(<graph>[, <option1>, <option2>, ...])* will draw the graph pictorially. The code snippet below shows this in action:

```
$ maxima -q
(%i1) load(graphs)$
...
0 errors, 0 warnings
(%i2) g: create_graph([0, 1], [[0, 1]])$
(%i3) dg: create_graph([0, 1], [[0, 1]], directed=true)$
(%i4) draw_graph(g, show_id=true, vertex_size=5, vertex_
color=yellow)$
(%i5) draw_graph(dg, show_id=true, vertex_size=5, vertex_
color=yellow)$
```

The '*show_id=true*' option draws the vertex numbers, and *vertex_size* and *vertex_color* draw the vertices with the corresponding size and colour.

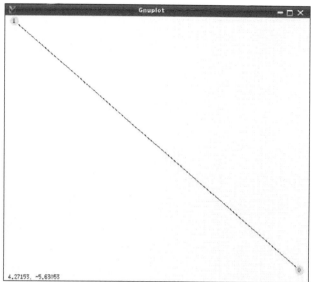

Figure 1: A simple undirected graph

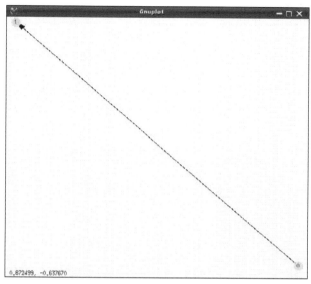

Figure 2: A simple directed graph

Note that a graph without any duplicate edges and without any loops is called a simple graph. Also, an edge from a vertex U to V is not a duplicate of an edge from vertex V to U in a directed graph but is considered a duplicate in an undirected graph. Maxima's package supports only simple graphs, i.e., graphs without duplicate edges and loops.

A simple graph can also be equivalently represented by adjacency of vertices, which means by lists of adjacent vertices for every vertex. *print_graph(<graph>)* exactly displays those lists. The following code, in continuation from the previous code snippet, demonstrates this:

```
(%i6) print_graph(g)$

Graph on 2 vertices with 1 edges.
Adjacencies:
  1 :  0
  0 :  1
(%i7) print_graph(dg)$

Digraph on 2 vertices with 1 arcs.
Adjacencies:
  1 :
  0 :  1
(%i8) quit();
```

create_graph(<num_of_vertices>, <edge_list>[, directed]) is another way of creating a graph using *create_graph()*. Here, the vertices are created as *0, 1, ..., <num_of_vertices> - 1*. So, both the above graphs could equivalently be created as follows:

```
(%i1) load(graphs)$
...
0 errors, 0 warnings
```

```
(%i2) g: create_graph(2, [[0, 1]]);
(%o2)                    GRAPH(2 vertices, 1 edges)
(%i3) dg: create_graph(2, [[0, 1]], directed=true);
(%o3)                    DIGRAPH(2 vertices, 1 arcs)
(%i4) quit();
```

make_graph(<vertices>, <predicate>[, directed]) is another interesting way of creating a graph, based on vertex connectivity conditions specified by the *<predicate>* function. *<vertices>* could be an integer or a set/list of vertices. If it is a positive integer, then the vertices would be *1, 2, ..., <vertices>*. In any case, *<predicate>* should be a function taking two arguments of the vertex type and returning true or false. *make_graph()* creates a graph with the vertices specified as above, and with the edges between the vertices, for which the *<predicate>* function returns true.

A simple case would be, if the *<predicate>* always returns true, then it would create a complete graph, i.e., a simple graph where all vertices are connected to each other. Here are a couple of demonstrations of *make_graph()*:

```
$ maxima -q
(%i1) load(graphs)$
...
0 errors, 0 warnings
(%i2) f(i, j) := true$
(%i3) g: make_graph(6, f);
(%o3)                  GRAPH(6 vertices, 15 edges)
(%i4) draw_graph(g, show_id=true, vertex_color=yellow)$
(%i5) f(i, j) := is(mod(i, j)=0)$
(%i6) g: make_graph(10, f, directed = true);
(%o6)                 DIGRAPH(10 vertices, 17 arcs)
(%i7) draw_graph(g, show_id=true, vertex_color=yellow, vertex_
size=4)$
(%i8) quit();
```

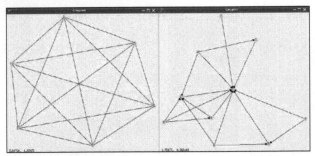

Figure 3: More simple graphs

Figure 3 shows the output graphs from the above code.

Graph varieties

Those aware of graphs will know or at least have heard of a variety of them. Here's a list of some of them, available in Maxima's graphs package (through functions):

- Empty graph *(empty_graph(n))* – A graph with a given 'n' vertices but no edges.
- Complete graph *(complete_graph(n))* – A simple graph with all possible edges for a given 'n' vertices.
- Complete bipartite graph *(complete_bipartite_graph(m, n))* – A simple graph with two sets of vertices, having all possible edges between the vertices from the two sets, but with no edge between the vertices of the same set.
- Cube graph *(cube_graph(n))* – A graph representing an n-dimensional cube.
- Dodecahedron graph *(dodecahedron_graph())* – A graph forming a 3-D polyhedron with 12 pentagonal faces.
- Cuboctahedron graph *(cuboctahedron_graph())* – A graph forming a 3-D polyhedron with eight triangular faces and 12 square faces.
- Icosahedron graph *(icosahedron_graph())* – A graph forming a 3-D polyhedron with 20 triangular faces.
- Icosidodecahedron graph *(icosidodecahedron_graph())* – A graph forming a 3-D uniform star polyhedron with 12 star faces and 20 triangular faces.

And here follows a demonstration of the above, along with the visuals *(left to right, top to bottom)* in Figure 4:

```
$ maxima -q
(%i1) load(graphs)$

...

0 errors, 0 warnings
(%i2) g: empty_graph(5);
(%o2)                    GRAPH(5 vertices, 0 edges)
(%i3) draw_graph(g, show_id=true, vertex_color=yellow)$
(%i4) g: complete_graph(5);
(%o4)                    GRAPH(5 vertices, 10 edges)
(%i5) draw_graph(g, show_id=true, vertex_color=yellow)$
(%i6) g: complete_bipartite_graph(5, 3);
(%o6)                    GRAPH(8 vertices, 15 edges)
(%i7) draw_graph(g, show_id=true, vertex_color=yellow)$
(%i8) g: cube_graph(3);
```

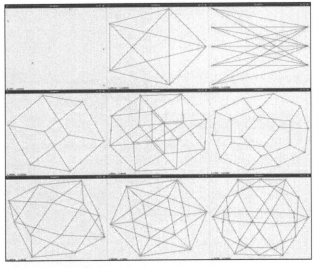

Figure 4: Graph varieties

```
(%o8)                    GRAPH(8 vertices, 12 edges)
(%i9) draw_graph(g, show_id=true, vertex_color=yellow)$
(%i10) g: cube_graph(4);
(%o10)                   GRAPH(16 vertices, 32 edges)
(%i11) draw_graph(g, show_id=true, vertex_color=yellow)$
(%i12) g: dodecahedron_graph();
(%o12)                   GRAPH(20 vertices, 30 edges)
(%i13) draw_graph(g, show_id=true, vertex_color=yellow)$
(%i14) g: cuboctahedron_graph();
(%o14)                   GRAPH(12 vertices, 24 edges)
(%i15) draw_graph(g, show_id=true, vertex_color=yellow)$
(%i16) g: icosahedron_graph();
(%o16)                   GRAPH(12 vertices, 30 edges)
(%i17) draw_graph(g, show_id=true, vertex_color=yellow)$
(%i18) g: icosidodecahedron_graph();
(%o18)                   GRAPH(30 vertices, 60 edges)
(%i19) draw_graph(g, show_id=true, vertex_color=yellow)$
(%i20) quit();
```

Graph beauties

Graphs are really beautiful to visualise. Some of the many beautiful graphs available in Maxima's graphs package (through functions) are listed below:

- Circulant graph *(circulant_graph(n, [x, y, ...]))* – A graph with vertices *0, ..., n-1*, where every vertex is adjacent to its xth, y^{th}, ... vertices. Visually, it has a cyclic group of symmetries.
- Flower graph *(flower_snark(n))* – A graph like a flower with 'n' petals and 4*n vertices.
- Wheel graph *(wheel_graph(n))* – A graph like a wheel with 'n' vertices.
- Clebsch graph *(clebsch_graph())* – Another symmetrical graph beauty, named by J J Seidel.
- Frucht graph *(frucht_graph())* – A graph with 12 vertices, 18 edges and no non-trivial symmetries, such that every vertex has three neighbours. It is named after Robert Frucht.

- Grötzsch graph *(grotzch_graph())* – A triangle-free graph with 11 vertices and 20 edges, named after Herbert Grötzsch.
- Heawood graph *(heawood_graph())* – A symmetrical graph with 14 vertices and 21 edges, named after Percy John Heawood.
- Petersen graph *(petersen_graph())* – A symmetrical graph with 10 vertices and 15 edges, named after Julius Petersen.
- Tutte graph *(tutte_graph())* – A graph with 46 vertices and 69 edges, such that every vertex has three neighbours. It is named after W T Tutte.

And here follows a demonstration of some of the above, along with the visuals (left to right, top to bottom) in Figure 5:

```
$ maxima -q
(%i1) load(graphs)$
...
0 errors, 0 warnings
(%i2) g: circulant_graph(10, [1, 3]);
(%o2)                    GRAPH(10 vertices, 20 edges)
(%i3) draw_graph(g, show_id=true, vertex_color=yellow)$
(%i4) g: circulant_graph(10, [1, 3, 4, 6]);
(%o4)                    GRAPH(10 vertices, 40 edges)
(%i5) draw_graph(g, show_id=true, vertex_color=yellow)$
(%i6) g: flower_snark(3);
(%o6)                    GRAPH(12 vertices, 18 edges)
(%i7) draw_graph(g, show_id=true, vertex_color=yellow)$
(%i8) g: flower_snark(5);
(%o8)                    GRAPH(20 vertices, 30 edges)
(%i9) draw_graph(g, show_id=true, vertex_color=yellow)$
(%i10) g: flower_snark(8);
(%o10)                   GRAPH(32 vertices, 48 edges)
(%i11) draw_graph(g, show_id=true, vertex_color=yellow)$
(%i12) g: flower_snark(10);
(%o12)                   GRAPH(40 vertices, 60 edges)
(%i13) draw_graph(g, show_id=true, vertex_color=yellow)$
(%i14) g: wheel_graph(3);
(%o14)                   GRAPH(4 vertices, 6 edges)
(%i15) draw_graph(g, show_id=true, vertex_color=yellow)$
(%i16) g: wheel_graph(4);
(%o16)                   GRAPH(5 vertices, 8 edges)
(%i17) draw_graph(g, show_id=true, vertex_color=yellow)$
(%i18) g: wheel_graph(5);
(%o18)                   GRAPH(6 vertices, 10 edges)
(%i19) draw_graph(g, show_id=true, vertex_color=yellow)$
(%i20) g: wheel_graph(10);
(%o20)                   GRAPH(11 vertices, 20 edges)
(%i21) draw_graph(g, show_id=true, vertex_color=yellow)$
(%i22) g: wheel_graph(100);
(%o22)                   GRAPH(101 vertices, 200 edges)
(%i23) draw_graph(g, show_id=true, vertex_color=yellow)$
(%i24) g: clebsch_graph();
(%o24)                   GRAPH(16 vertices, 40 edges)
(%i25) draw_graph(g, show_id=true, vertex_color=yellow)$
(%i26) g: grotzch_graph();
```

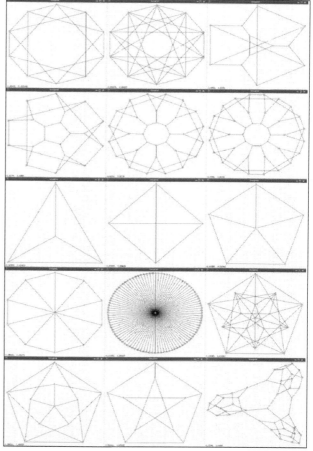

Figure 5: Graph beauties

```
(%o26)                   GRAPH(11 vertices, 20 edges)
(%i27) draw_graph(g, show_id=true, vertex_color=yellow)$
(%i28) g: petersen_graph();
(%o28)                   GRAPH(10 vertices, 15 edges)
(%i29) draw_graph(g, show_id=true, vertex_color=yellow)$
(%i30) g: tutte_graph();
(%o30)                   GRAPH(46 vertices, 69 edges)
(%i31) draw_graph(g, show_id=true, vertex_color=yellow)$
(%i32) quit();
```

What next?

You may be wondering what to do with all these visualisations, apart from just staring at them. Visualisations were just to motivate you. In fact, every graph has a particular set of properties, which distinguishes it from the other. And, there is a lot of beautiful mathematics involved in these properties. If you are motivated enough, try playing around with these graphs and their properties. **END**

By: Anil Kumar Pugalia

The author is a gold medallist from NIT Warangal and IISc Bengaluru. Mathematics and knowledge sharing are two of his many passions. Learn more about him at *http://sysplay.in*. He can be reached at *email@sarika-pugs.com*.

"Jolla offers something new and fresh, and a lot of people love it!"

If you are someone who likes trying out something new, check out the Jolla smartphone. This different, rather unconventional device has just been made available in India. The smartphone comes as a breath of fresh air from the makers of Meego and is based on open source technology. The best part is that the makers are not snooping on your data. *Diksha P Gupta* from *Open Source For You* caught up with *Marc Dillon, co-founder and chief operating officer, Jolla,* to discover more about what the new smartphone and operating system are all about, and to find out how Jolla differs from Android. Read on...

Marc Dillon, co-founder and chief operating officer, Jolla

Q **I understand that the Jolla team took a long time to develop this ecosystem after Meego had finished with it...do correct me if I'm wrong.**

We built the Jolla smartphone in six months because we were partners with ST Ericsson and we were ready to go into final production. But Ericsson changed its business so we had to start from scratch. We have been working on the operating system, but we essentially created this product in six months.

Q **How much of Jolla is Meego?**

We took some of the lower layers, and most importantly, the people, the passion and the thoughts about where to go forward. The Meego operating system that was left in the open source world had about a billion dollars' worth of investments. We took parts of it forward to create something that was new, with a new user interface, integration with QT—which is the framework for anyone to make a Sailfish (Jolla's OS) application, et al.

Q **So is this your first launch for Jolla mobile phones?**

In India, it is the first. We first launched in Finland last year, and then we went to places like Hong Kong and Kazakhstan. There are a couple of more launches coming up.

Q **What has the response and uptake for Sailfish been like, vis-a-vis the other open source platforms like Android, Firefox OS and Android One?**

First of all, Android isn't open any more. Google is closing things down, and it is getting increasingly more closed. There are a lot of restrictions on what you can do with Google's code. The company has a lot of licensing terms and things like that.

Firefox's mobile OS is a kind of low-end thing, with no standard for HTML5, which is the basis of the UI. Firefox is targeting the lower end of the market, as opposed to what we are trying to do. I think that we have a high-end user experience at a reasonable price. The hardware is more than good enough to be able to have all your applications open all the time.

Google may market its phones in different ways, but basically, all its phones are the same. If manufacturers want to create something new, they either push the price point down (which makes it difficult for them to make money) or they make luxury, high-end phones. Since there is nothing much that they can do to the software, manufacturers have to do something to the hardware to make it different, which is quite a challenge. However, we are different inside out. So, allowing the users to multitask, without selling their data; giving them the capability to use the phone comfortably with one hand; and other such features are the USPs of a Jolla smartphone. These unique features make a Jolla smartphone a very compelling device.

Q **That is great, but India is the kind of market that likes tried and tested stuff instead of experimenting with something new, unless it's from a huge brand. Sailfish is a pretty new player in the software ecosystem and you have not partnered with any brand on the hardware front either. Why?**

'Ecosystem' is a funny word! The term was created around marketing ideas like how many apps there are in a store, but one has to understand that there are only a few that are important to everyone, and then there are a few that are important to a specific set of people. A person doesn't need 800,000 applications. So, the first thing we had looked at was our Android compatibility. There is zero Android in our device, out-of-the-box, but you can still get any of your favourite Android-based applications on a Jolla smartphone.

Q How would one run an Android application on a Jolla smartphone?

We have several Android app stores, which can be accessed from the Jolla store that is pre-installed on the device. You can download the official versions of your favourite apps via this app store. Precisely what it means is that you can run any Android application on the Jolla operating system. The other thing about an 'ecosystem' is that our software does run on pretty much any Android device. So, when we go and talk to a hardware partner, we walk in the door with our operating system running on their hardware. This is just a starting point. Due to this attribute of the Jolla OS, our discussions with hardware partners are on a pretty aggressive level. There isn't anything to announce yet, but there will soon be other devices running the Sailfish OS system in the near future.

Q In what ways is the Sailfish OS better than Android?

We pledge not to sell users' private data, which is the most important thing. Android was designed to take users' data and turn that into something that the company can make money with.

According to certain studies, typical users pick up their phone about 200 times a day. So, in such a scenario, multi-tasking is extremely important. Multi-tasking means the ability to see everything on the screen that is important to you and, hopefully, be able to react to those notifications. You only need one processor core in order to read your email, text messages and do all such things. With our phone's two cores, you can run lots of applications at the same time and leave them all open.

The other thing is that Jolla smartphones allow one-handed usage. People generally use both hands on their devices, even while walking, but with Jolla, you can do everything that you need to do with just one hand. So if you have the other hand holding on to a bus railing or carrying a bag, you can easily operate your Jolla smartphone.

So these three things—privacy, a great UI for multi-tasking and one-handed usage keep Jolla ahead and different from Android.

Q So why would someone who is very accustomed to using Android switch to Jolla?

Every time you pick up a phone, there are a lot of things you do. One example is sending a text message. Try doing that with your phone and observe how many times you have to actually touch the device; how many times you have to look at it, and mess with it to be able to do what really should be effortless. So you spend a tremendous amount of time with your device everyday, but does this give you the best experience, or do you feel like you have to do a lot of different things to get the most of every action you do, on a daily basis? For us, it is about providing the fastest and the easiest ways to control and handle your digital life. That is one of the most compelling aspects of a Jolla smartphone. The user experience in an Android device is five years old and it hasn't changed much over

Specifications of the Jolla smartphone	
Dimensions and weight	Height: 131 mm Width: 68 mm Thickness: 9.9 mm Weight: 141 g
Processor	Qualcomm Dual Core 1.4GHz
Network and connectivity	GSM: 850/900/1800/1900MHz WCDMA: 900/2100MHz (Bands 1/8) 4G LTE 800/1800/2600MHz (Bands 3/7/20)* WLAN802.11 b/g/n 2.4GHz Bluetooth 4.0 EDR HS AGPS and GLONASS USB 2.0 HS Standard 3.5 mm 4-pin audio jack Micro SIM Standard MicroUSB connectivity and charging Extension interfaces for wireless NFC, power in/out and I2C data connectivity
Memory	16GB storage 1GB RAM MicroSD slot
Display	Ample 11.43 cm IPS qHD (960×540) display 5-point multi-touch with Gorilla 2 glass
Camera	8MP AF camera with LED flash 2MP front-facing camera
Sensors	Proximity Accelerometer Gyro E-compass Ambient light
Power	Approximate talk and standby time: 9-10 hrs (GSM/3G) and 500 hrs User-replaceable battery (2100mAh, 3.8V, 7.98Wh)

* LTE wireless service may not be available even if listed bands are supported by your carrier.

that period, while we offer something that is much faster. It is much more efficient, much easier to use and much more powerful.

Q Which current operating system do you look up to when adding features in Jolla?

It's interesting, but I think the others have taken a lot from us. At the moment, we are primarily working with our customers and our consumers in order to continue to deliver things that they want. So we design this in the beginning for ourselves, and then we take feedback from our customers and even potential customers and continue to deliver new things for them. I don't understand why people refrain from trying out something new, particularly in the smartphone space. If we just had Chevrolet and Toyota, would that be enough? We offer something new and fresh, and a lot of people really love it. **END**

Pegasystems Plans to Double its Headcount of Developers in India!

India's vast pool of developers represents an attractive business proposition to many multinational firms, and Pegasystems Inc is no exception. This US-based company entered India in 2007, with the idea of hiring the best talent from the developer community. Pegasystems has grown since then. The company has its strategies in place as India remains one of its key focus areas. *Kamya Kandhari* from the *Open Source For You* team caught up with *Mike Pyle, senior vice president, engineering, Pegasystems Inc,* at the firm's recently concluded Pega Developers' Conference and discussed its plans for expanding its development facility in the country. Excerpts:

Mike Pyle, senior vice president, engineering, Pegasystems Inc

Q Pegasystems has been organising the Pega Developers' Conference for two years now, to engage with the developers working on the company's technologies. What is your strategy to reach out to the developers, apart from organising events like these?

Well, we do a lot. We participate in the Java One conference, either as speakers, showcase our products, or have an information booth. Essentially, we would like to evaluate and participate in any kind of technology forum to engage with the developers' community in India.

Q With trends like SMAC (social, mobile, analytics and cloud) coming in, how has the life of a developer changed?

The array of technology that they need to understand has become bigger. The mobile, in particular, has caused a lot of confusion. The iOS platform is pretty mature and well organised. The Android platform, on the other hand, has a lot of variations, with different versions and it is very difficult to produce something that will work with every target device that somebody may show up with. BlackBerry has some adoption, but one of the big problems is to produce something for a target audience even when we have no control over the kinds of devices and software that they are going to use. In general, there are a number of technologies involved in building any serious application and it's very hard for one person to have expertise across the array. It's hard to co-ordinate and make everything work together in the way that's needed. It's a big challenge for people, so one of the things that we try to do is pull a lot of these technologies onto our platform. That way, if you learn the platform, you can at least get the basic application working and then you can enhance it in particular areas using special skills, if you want to.

Q A recent survey conducted by EMC suggests that there is a dearth of talent in India when it comes to the latest technologies for the mobile and the cloud. Do you agree?

There is a dearth of talent on the planet when it comes to those technologies! So why would India be any different? It's very hard to find people with a lot of experience. You can't find people with a lot of experience in a technology that is very new. I think India has an advantage as most of it is just mathematics. You produce so many engineers; you have so much talent here. It's a very aggressive and energetic community. Whenever I come to India, and I do so at least four times a year, I notice a huge surge in energy levels here.

The average age of our employees in India is way younger than the average age of our employees across the globe. That just gives India a tremendous advantage with which it is going to catch up. The Indian developers' community is going to be able to grow with the number of people who have the skills and experience faster than other people will grow because India has the numbers on its side.

> "The open source community has matured a lot in the last few years and some of the technologies have been used by companies like Google, which has been great in injecting some discipline into the open source arena, to the extent that open source is now leading the way in providing a really good disciplined practice for developing software."

Pega has always regarded India not as a back office but as an R&D centre, and we believe in leveraging the people that we have here, to innovate. Our vice president emphasises how important the UI is, and most of our UI developers are in India. We have one team in Cambridge and the rest of our four to five teams for the UI are in India. Many of those teams have been with us since we opened office in India. Our No 1 employee is a UI engineer and she joined us on Day One. The experience and skills that we have here is a very fundamental part of engineering. So I think India is very well placed in terms of talent.

Q How have all these technologies affected or modified the development process in your company?

We have had to learn these technologies ourselves. We made a strategic move last year when we realised how important the mobile was. We looked around for a company that was well placed in the mobile space, which we could acquire to give us the kind of jumpstart in mobile technology. So we acquired Antenna Software – a leader in mobile technology. It has a huge operation in Bengaluru, and that's now a part of the Pega R&D centre in the city. We have had about a 100 people join us from Antenna and that gave us a big leg up. The acquisition comes with a whole new talent tool kit in terms of designing, debugging and integrating.

Our approach has always been to bring technology into the model. Our model is to encourage people to build on our platform. So we have had to adapt the model to embrace mobile concepts. It is very easy to project the application on to a mobile device and is no different than projecting it on a big screen. You just have to use a responsive UI but if you want some of the native capabilities, then you have to combine it into a hybrid model. We have been able to do that and integrate it with our model. So we have a lot of our engineers exposed to mobile device native programming, which is a whole new realm.

The other big change that we have started to see is in the open source community. The open source community has matured a lot in the last few years and some of the technologies have been used by companies like Google,

> " The reason we are in India is because we have great talent here. As long as we continue to find great talent in Hyderabad, we will continue to grow in that city and the same is true for Bengaluru."

which has been great in injecting some discipline into the open source arena, to the extent that open source is now leading the way in providing a really good disciplined practice for developing software. So, lots of companies, including Pega, have started adopting these practices.

Q How has your hiring pattern changed over the past one year, as there has been a spurt of new technologies?

I wouldn't say that it has changed radically, though it may have accelerated in certain areas. We have our core development people who build our core enterprise platform but we also have developers who build products on this platform in various business areas, for example, in healthcare, communications, insurance, financial services, etc. We have made some investments in growing the applications side of the business last year. We have accelerated hiring people who are building applications and some of those people are probably less technical. We bring people from a business background so they understand insurance, financial services and communications. They can use our platform because it is so easy to use that people don't necessarily need to have a computer science degree.

There is a company in the US that specialises in taking people who do not have a computer science background. These people are majors in philosophy, music, English, etc, but they are smart people. One of the advantages is that today, everybody who comes out of college has some exposure to computers and technology. They take these people and they train them in Pega technology and then they put them to work in Pega development projects. This means they make a lot more money than they would as music or English majors. Also, there is a shortage of people who have Pega skills in the market. So this company does that very successfully. We have been talking with a few companies in India who are interested in doing the same thing. Hopefully, we will start to see some of that soon.

Q Last year, when my colleague met you at the same event, you had mentioned some of your expansion plans. How much have you expanded in the past one year?

In Bengaluru, we just opened a new floor. We had completely filled the space we had in Bengaluru because the Antenna acquisition brought in about 100 people. We acquired another company called MeshLabs, which does

social analytics. It monitors all social media channels and does a sentiment analysis—identifying whether the tweets are positive or negative; this is important as companies monitor tweets since they are looking for those who are unhappy with their products or services. That way, they can reach out and fix the problem, or if someone is happy, they can enhance their customer satisfaction levels. We have also continued to hire and grow the team in Bengaluru, where we now have between 200 to 300 people.

At Hyderabad, things are even more chaotic. Every inch of space in the office is packed because we have just grown and grown. We are just on the cusp of moving to a bigger facility—from the DLF building where we are currently, to a new building in Mindspace. This will give us the space to nearly double the capacity that we have in Hyderabad.

Q Apart from Hyderabad and Bengaluru, do you plan to expand to other cities in India?

No, not at this moment. The reason we are in India is because we have great talent here. As long as we continue to find great talent in Hyderabad, we will continue to grow in that city and the same is true for Bengaluru. If there is some compelling reason to go somewhere else, then we are open to it. But having a presence in multiple locations means we have to co-ordinate and make people feel connected, which as a company we are very good at, but we are also careful when we do that.

Q By how much do you plan to increase your developers strength in the coming years?

It is tough to say…we are planning for a capacity that is double our current level. We don't have a timeframe as to when it will happen but one of our primary focus areas is growth in India.

Q With the arrival of the new technologies mentioned earlier, how has your hiring pattern changed with respect to freshers?

We run an internship programme, courtesy which, last year we took on 25 people. We take them as interns in their last year, they work for us and then they become part of Pega. We do pay them stipends and when they graduate, they come and work for us.

Q In this conference, you seem to have restricted yourself to the developers of the companies that are your customers. As I believe, there is a big community of third party and independent developers in India. So why aren't you focusing on them? And if you are targeting them, how do you plan to tap them?

Well, for the first time this year, we ran the Java developers' session at the Pega Developers' Conference. So, the people who came for this session have no experience working with Pega at all. They are not our customers; though they may work for some customers.

We reached out and said that Pega people get paid more; so anybody who has heard of Pega and wants to join the ecosystem can be a part of this session. The session was geared towards bringing people who don't know what Pega is all about and teaching them about us. Participants actually got to build a live application in the session. It was pretty well received. Also, we participate in various industry conferences and try and be active within the community to let people know what we are doing.

Q You just mentioned how open source technologies have evolved over the years. How much of the development process in Pega involves open source technologies?

We use quite a lot of open source technologies like XSLT transformation. One of the things to do before releasing a product is to make sure that all of the licensing is correct. We use scanner software to do that. We would also like to contribute more to open source. It's something we have never really engaged in as a company in the past, but many of our engineers contribute to open source. One of the things that we are looking forward to doing in the coming years, as a company, is probably engage much more in open source.

Q Do you see open source technologies evolving and overtaking proprietary development processes, because of trends like SMAC?

It's going to be a very big thing. There are enough interesting models on open source which make it worthwhile. When a company commercialises an open source version of software, the commercial version is generally inexpensive enough for us to find it attractive. So we use Linux, Postgres and OpenStack, which are open source projects but there are commercial companies that have versions of those technologies. This duality model is really going to drive things forward -- maybe much faster than in the past, as there is some reluctance in taking up entirely open source modules. People will take individual modules and plug them in to their model as, in worst case scenarios, they can fix it themselves.

> "We would also like to contribute more to open source. It's something we have never really engaged in as a company in the past, but many of our engineers contribute to open source. One of the things that we are looking forward to doing in the coming years, as a company, is probably engage much more in open source."

Q The Indian government is focusing a lot on setting up manufacturing companies in India, which 'Make in India'. How do you view the policies of the new Indian government?

I love that idea because we make most of everything in India. The IT minister today was talking about what the government of Telangana is doing—it wants to invest in technology with a programme called Digital India. I think this is a tremendous programme. India is important to us as a market, as it is growing so rapidly with so many people; the standard of living is increasing. We don't have many customers in India though. Vodafone India is a customer of ours, which does all its outbound marketing using Pega technology, through which we are directly touching the Indian customers.

The other one is PayPal, which also has a large customer base in India. We have our technologies being used by companies operating in India. But there is a much bigger opportunity here. India is not a sales market for us yet, but we keep looking at it. One opportunity that we see is to work with the state governments or the Indian government on some sort of initiatives. If it has a social benefit and if we find the right application, we could do it as a social outreach activity. That would be an interesting thing to look at but there is nothing tangible to it as yet. END

TIPS & TRICKS

 Use hashtags to simplify searching for commands

We use hashtags all over in Twitter. They are excellent for discovering and tagging long text. A # in the shell is used to comment a line. Hashtags can also make our workflow more productive. Let's see how this happens.

We normally type very long commands in our Bash shell and it becomes difficult to search for the same command from History. Here is a simple trick that will make searching easier. All you need to do is to append a hashtag at the end of every command you type. And later search for the hashtag in *reverse-i-search (Ctrl + R)*. Adding a # at the end of the command will not affect the execution of the command since anything that follows # is treated as a comment in Bash—the text is silently ignored after #.

Let us understand the above procedure using an example.

Let us assume that I run the following command on my Bash shell:

```
$ tar xzvf filename #untar
```

Now, just press *Ctrl + R* in the terminal window and type *untar;* you will get the above command from the Bash history of commands.

— *Sudhanshu Mishra,*
mrsud94@gmail.com

Delete files that are x days old

Sometimes in Linux, you want to clear out older files in a directory. One example could be if you have a security system and it continuously writes video files to a directory on your NAS (Network Attached Storage) until it fills it up. You've figured out that if you keep a week's collection of videos, there will be plenty of space for other users. So, here is a command that will delete all files that are older than seven days. Do remember to execute this command with caution as it can delete your important data if not used correctly:

```
#find /path/to/files/ -type f -mtime +7 -exec rm -rf {} \;
```

Let us look at the above command more closely.

find: This is the command that will search for the files.
/path/to/files/: This is the top level directory to start searching.

-type f: This ensures we don't remove directories, but only files.

-mtime +7: Removes files older than '7' days. Change to '+14' to delete files older than two weeks.

-exec: This indicates what to do with the files we found.

rm -rf: Removes the files recursively and forcefully.

{}: This represents each file we find.

\;: This is the end of the exec.

On successfully testing the above command you can create a *cron* job to automate the process. The *cron* job entry given below in the *crontab* file will execute the above command every night at 2 a.m. and delete all files older than 7 days in the folder.

```
2 * * * /bin/find /path/to/files/ -type f -mtime +7 -exec rm
-rf {} \;
```

— *Ninad Shaha, ninadshaha@iitb.ac.in*

How to resize a Linux partition

This tip will help you to resize your partition easily in a few steps, without the need to reinstall the operating system again.

> **Note:** It is recommended to take backups of all the files.

Open up a terminal and run the following command:

```
$ sudo init 1
```

The *'init'* command will load *runlevel 1,* which is used to carry out administrative operations like maintenance or emergency repairs.

Here, we are going to extend the root partition using free space from the home partition to make space for data in the root folder. The partitions should be a logical volume (which is more flexible than other partition schemes) and of file system type *ext3/ext4.*

Inside *runlevel 1* run the following commands:

```
$ cd /
$ umount /home
```

Here, we are changing our directory to root so that we can unmount */home* and modify the partition's size.

```
$ e2fsck -f /dev/debian/home
```

Run *e2fsck*, a file system check utility that checks for bad sectors and I/O errors related to HDD. This helps in fixing errors in the file system.

```
$ resize2fs /dev/debian/home 'size'G
$ lvresize -L 'size'G /dev/debian/home
```

Replace 'size' with the value of your choice (in GB). This will shrink or resize the */home* partition to the specified 'size'.

```
$ mount -a
```

This command will mount all the partitions mentioned in *fstab (/etc/fstab). fstab* lists all the available disks and disk partitions.

```
$ lvextend -L +'root_size'G /dev/debian/root
$ resize2fs /dev/debian/root
```

Here we are appending 'root_size' (in GB) to the root partition. Replace 'root_size' with the value you want to append to the root partition.

```
$ init 5
```

The above command will restart the system normally. Now, you have successfully resized your partition without reinstalling the operating system.

– Jackson Isaac, jacksonisaac2008@gmail.com

Know what everybody is up to on a shared server

On a shared server, we may want to know if anyone is doing something suspicious that is troubling others, like slowing down the machine. Run the following command:

```
#w
```

w displays information about the users currently on the machine and the processes they are using. The output is shown in the following order: the current time, how long the system has been running, how many users are currently logged on, and the system load averages for the past 1, 5 and 15 minutes.

– Madhusudana Y N, madhusudanayn@gmail.com

Is your server a physical or virtual machine?

Just suppose you do an SSH login to a GNU/Linux machine and would like to figure out whether it is a physical or a virtual machine. Here is a command that will disclose that status of the server:

```
#dmidecode
```

This command gives details of the hardware.

If it is a physical machine, then the output will display the product's name in a manner similar to what follows:

```
[bash]$ dmidecode | grep "Product"
Product Name: PowerEdge 1750
```

If it is a virtual machine, then the output will be something like this:

```
[bash]$ dmidecode | grep Product
        Product Name: VMware Virtual Platform
        Product Name: 440BX Desktop Reference Platform
```

– Narendra Kangralkar,
narendrakangralkar@gmail.com

Disable 'automatic image loading' in Firefox

Web browser users sometimes need to disable auto-loading of images to limit bandwidth consumption, examine untrusted websites and for a few more reasons. This has become difficult to accomplish with recent versions of the Firefox Web browser. But here's how you can do it:

1) Type 'about:config' in the Web address box of Firefox and hit 'Enter'.
2) Click the button labelled 'I'll be careful, I promise!'
3) Type 'permissions.default.image' in the search bar that appears below the address box.
4) Double-click the text '1' against the search result by the aforementioned key phrase 'permissions.default.image'.
5) Change the value from '1' to '2' and hit 'OK'.
6) Visit a site or close the tab.

To revert to auto-loading of images, just change the '2' back to '1' following a similar procedure. Please do not commit any typographic errors or the results can be disastrous!

—A Datta,
webmaster@aucklandwhich.org

DVD OF THE MONTH

Protect your IT infrastructure with BackBox Linux while you enjoy the power
of a BSD-based distro.

FreeBSD 9.3: FreeBSD is an advanced
computer operating system that is used to
power today's servers and desktops. It is best
known for its stability and security in server
environments.

GhostBSD 4.0: GhostBSD is a user-
friendly operating system based on FreeBSD.
GhostBSD is based on well designed and
thoroughly tested open source solutions, and
it creates an easy-to-use familiar workspace
for both the home and office/production
environments. The live environment can also be
used to rescue data.

BackBox 4.0 Live: This is an
Ubuntu-based Linux distribution that performs
penetration tests and security assessments.

R N I No. DELENG/2012/49440, Mailed on 27/28th of Advance month   Delhi Postal Regd. No. DL(S)-01/3443/2013-15
Published on 27th of Advance month

There is a place for Postgres in every datacenter.

WE CAN HELP YOU FIND IT.

Postgres delivers. Enterprise class Performance, Security, Success.
For 80% less.

EnterpriseDB - The Postgres Database Company

Sales-india@enterprisedb.com

EDB®
ENTERPRISEDB

EnterpriseDB Software India Pvt Ltd
Unit #3, Godrej Castlemaine
Pune - 411 01 India
T +91 20 30589500/01

Printed in Great Britain
by Amazon.co.uk, Ltd.,
Marston Gate.